MW00774649

The
Heroin User's
Handbook

The
Heroin User's
Handbook

by Francis Moraes, Ph.D.

Loompanics Unlimited
Port Townsend, Washington

Neither the author nor the publisher assumes any responsibility for the use or misuse of information contained in this book. It is sold for informational purposes only. Be Warned!

The Heroin User's Handbook
© 2001 by Francis Moraes, Ph.D.

Published by:
Loompanics Unlimited
PO Box 1197
Port Townsend, WA 98368
Loompanics Unlimited is a division of Loompanics Enterprises, Inc.
Phone: 360-385-2230
E-mail: service@loompanics.com
Web site: www.loompanics.com

Cover art by Craig Howell

ISBN 1-55950-216-9
Library of Congress Card Catalog Number 2001087354

Contents

Chapter One
  Dispelling Myths.. 1
  Don't Try Heroin; Heroin Is Just Morphine; Heroin
  Compared to Other Drugs; Why Heroin Is Illegal; Heroin
  Can Be Used Safely

Chapter Two
  Acquisition... 17
  Heroin Distribution; Acquirers; Scoring on the Street;
  Connections; A Caution

Chapter Three
  Ingestion... 35
  Overview; Injection; Snorting; Smoking; Purifying Heroin;
  Final Thoughts

Chapter Four
  Risks... 69
  Physical Addiction; Disease; Overdose; Final Thoughts

Chapter Five
   Legal Issues 95
   Not Getting Arrested; Dealing With Police; The Legal
   System; Lawyers; Jail; Court-Mandated Treatment; Final
   Thoughts

Chapter Six
   Social Issues...123
   People in Your Neighborhood; Lovers; Junkies; Dealers;
   The Making of a Junkie; Old Junkie Tales; The Social Drug

Chapter Seven
   Addiction...139
   Why Heroin Addiction Sucks; Warning Signs; An
   Overview of Detox Methods; Opioid Substitution;
   Medicated Detox; Cold Turkey; Detoxing Yourself; Staying
   Clean; Going Back

Chapter Eight
   Parting Words...167

Appendix A
   Glossary...171

Appendix B
   Recommended Reading 181
   Avoiding Drugs; Drugs; History; Medicine; Miscellaneous;
   Law; Psychology

About the Author

Francis Moraes is trained as a research physicist and chemist. He was a physics professor at Portland State University in Portland, Oregon, where he became interested in Portland's vibrant heroin subculture — Portland is the number two heroin city (after New York City) according to DEA statistics. He spent several years studying this subculture in Portland, Seattle, New York City, and the San Francisco Bay Area. Dr. Moraes, Ph.D. has conducted substantial academic and pharmacological research and is the author of *The Little Book of Heroin* (Ronin, 2000) and *The Little Book of Opium* (Ronin, 2001).

Check out his Web site: www.heroinhelper.com

Chapter One
Dispelling Myths

The intent of this book is to educate the reader about all aspects of the use of heroin and to dispel the major myths by replacing them with accurate information. There is so much misinformation surrounding heroin that it is important to confront the major myths about the drug right away. This misinformation causes unnecessary pain throughout society — it kills people and destroys the lives of many more than the users themselves.

Don't Try Heroin

In writing this book, it is not my aim to encourage you to use heroin — far from it. My experience with heroin has cost me a great deal and I am not alone. Involvement with heroin at this time in history is very dangerous, so let me start by trying to talk you out of ever trying this drug — if you haven't already.

I know what you've heard: heroin is so good that if you try it once, you'll never stop. You have to remember, however, that pretty much everything you "know" about heroin comes from two sources: government propaganda and screenplays. Information from the government is at best misleading and at worst maliciously dishonest. Screenplays are fiction; they may provide correct information but they are more likely to be highly misleading. Be skeptical of any information you possess about heroin.

Reason One: Heroin Makes You Sick

For the vast majority of new users, heroin's primary effect is nausea. Many people become painfully ill for hours. It's not uncommon for a person to vomit five or more times from a single dose of the drug. Most people eventually get over the nausea and experience heroin's euphoric effects. For some of these people the nausea is an acceptable price to pay for the euphoria — for others, it is not.

Reason Two: Heroin High is Subtle

Aside from the possible nausea, the new user may be unhappy with heroin because of its rather subtle effects. At its best, heroin fills the user with a sense of contentment and this is surprisingly easy to miss by users who are expecting to be "smacked." No group seems to be more dissatisfied with its effects than regular pot smokers who are used to a high, which is in no sense subtle.

Don't fall for the line that a heroin rush is like a body-wide orgasm. The only time I've ever heard this is when it is coming from fictional characters or heroin "researchers" who have never taken the drug.

Reason Three: Heroin Can Kill You

So there are two practical reasons for not even trying heroin: it will probably make you sick and even if it doesn't, you might not notice the "high" or get any feeling of euphoria. You might still think it is worth a try. You might get sick or waste a few dollars, so what? A bigger issue, however, is that you could die.

In Chapter Four, I will discuss sudden death associated with heroin use. The problem with this is that it is not at all clear as to why this happens. There are precautions that can be taken, but it is still possible to end up dead. Roughly a thousand users die in this way each year.

Reason Four: Jail

Involvement with heroin can also result in terrible legal problems. I have peppered this book with the fact that much of the harm that heroin causes in the lives of its users comes from its legal status. Heroin is not just illegal; it is very illegal. Even the attempted possession of it is a felony.

If you are caught trying to buy it or possess it, you won't be handed a ticket, you will be handcuffed. If you were caught in a car, it will be towed and very likely seized to fund the "War on Drugs." You will be taken to jail. If it is your first "offense," you may end up in some kind of drug treatment program, which may require that you quit your job because of all of the "treatment sessions" and court appearances that take place during the day. If not this, you will end up with a felony conviction, which can put you in jail for many years. In the opinion of prospective employers (and landlords and the guy who cooks your Big Mac), the label "convicted felon" puts you in the same category as child molesters and murderers.

If you want a scary but very accurate account of just what you open yourself up for when you do illegal drugs, you should read *Drug Warriors and Their Prey* by Richard Lawrence Miller. In this book, Miller shows that in modern America, illegal drug users are being treated and used just as Jews were in Nazi Germany. By becoming an illegal drug user, you begin a process that ends in your destruction. The process is identification (drug testing), ostracism (job loss under most circumstances), concentration (arrest), and annihilation.

We haven't arrived at the annihilation ("final solution") phase yet. But I have heard politicians and pundits call for the death penalty for illegal drug users. Most notable is the former Los Angeles Chief of Police Daryl Gates' statement before Congress, "All casual drug users should be taken out and shot."[1] This should give

---

[1] What is more amazing is that these words created very little dissent. Gates' point was that we are at war (Drug War) and that drug users are traitors. In general, America's response was: good point!

you some idea of the hatred that doing any illegal drug, particularly heroin, will unleash upon you.

Reason Five: Heroin Catch-22

For me, none of these reasons — illness, subtlety of effect, death, and jail — compares to the fifth reason for not trying heroin. This is what I like to call the Heroin Catch-22:

- **If you don't like heroin** then you wasted your time and money.
- **If you do like heroin** then you are in danger of allowing heroin to become the most important thing in your life. This is how heroin can become very dangerous.

Any time you allow something to become the most important thing in your life, you put yourself in a dangerous position. The question is, what are you willing to do to get this thing? A person who likes heroin finds himself in a very difficult situation once he becomes addicted. It is one thing to fight the urge to do a drug that makes him feel good — this may be difficult, but even if he succeeds in this endeavor, he has another battle to fight. When he stops, he finds that he is physically sick. This can make him frantic, which can lead to his making choices that he would never before have thought possible.

It takes a great deal of discipline to use heroin without becoming addicted. This is because heroin is an addictive drug. Most heroin addicts that I have met do not have what most people would call addictive personalities. The fact of the matter is that if you do heroin enough, you will become physically addicted; it doesn't matter who you are.

Just being a heroin user has the effect of cutting you off from the rest of society because of the opinions that the majority of society holds regarding heroin. Few people who do not smoke marijuana will have a problem with you if you do. This is not the case with heroin. If you use heroin, you will be forced to hide it from everyone except those who also use it.

This book contains a great deal of information, which will be of interest to people who do not use and do not intend to use heroin. In a weird kind of way, this book will do more to keep people *off* heroin than all of the evil and misinformed anti-drug propaganda littering the bookstores and libraries of America. The reason is simple: I provide the reader with objective information about heroin. A brief perusal will show that using heroin takes a lot of work and that it is simply not worth it to the vast majority of people.

If you are already a user or you have already decided that you want to become a user, this book can be profoundly helpful. The saddest fact of heroin is that most users don't know any more than what the screenwriters and propagandists have told them. As a result, many heroin users become addicts who normally might not. And, when it comes to heroin, misinformation can mean death.

Heroin Is Just Morphine

Heroin is a narcotic. There are a lot of definitions of the word "narcotic." The most common is that a narcotic is any illegal drug. For the time being, I am interested in the medical definition of this word. Narcotics are defined by the highly useful, if governmentally biased, *The Encyclopedia of Drug Abuse* as "central nervous system depressants with analgesic and sedative properties." Analgesic is medical shorthand for a drug which relieves pain without loss of consciousness.

All opiates are derived from the opium poppy. From the opium poppy we get, with little work, opium. The primary ingredients in opium are morphine and codeine. Codeine will get you high, but it is a relatively poor high compared to that of morphine, and since morphine is the largest constituent of opium, it is reasonable to say that when one ingests opium he is doing so primarily to get the morphine.

The human body has opiate receptor sites. These sites are in the brain, spinal cord, intestines, and other areas that recognize opiates and tell the brain to feel the way opiates make a user feel: content and safe. The body produces its own morphine-like substances called opiate peptides or endorphins. These substances seem to be used by the body to control pain and mood. In other words, morphine stimulates the same parts of the body that are normally stimulated in your brain when you feel happy. This may be a primary reason why morphine itself has relatively few deleterious effects on the human body even after long use.

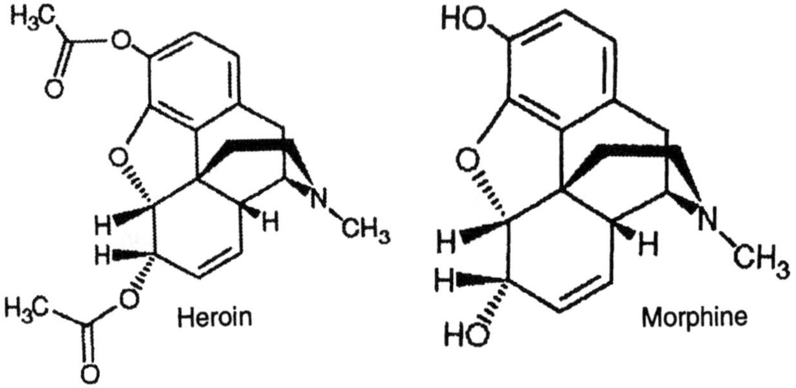

Figure 1
Heroin and morphine have almost identical chemical structures.

Heroin is created by combining morphine with acetic anhydride. Chemically, this converts the morphine into diacetylmorphine, which is just the morphine molecule with a couple of diacetyl groups tacked on. Figure 1 shows the similarities. Once in the body, chemicals strip away these diacetyl groups and turn the heroin back into morphine. This process takes place very quickly: heroin has a halflife[2] of about three minutes in the human body. Heroin itself does not affect the body. It is only after heroin has been converted into morphine that it becomes effective. Heroin is only a transport chemical — an effective way of getting morphine to the brain.

Heroin is more potent than morphine because it crosses over the blood-brain barrier — the separation between the circulatory system and the brain — more quickly than morphine. This fact has been mistakenly taken to mean that heroin has a greater rush asso-

---

[2] The halflife is the amount of time it takes the body to remove half of the substance. So in the case of heroin, after three minutes, only half of the amount ingested is still present. After six minutes, only a quarter is present. 9 minutes; 1/8; 12 minutes; 1/16; and so on.

ciated with it than morphine. This is not the case. It means that for an equal concentration in the blood, three heroin molecules will cross the blood-brain barrier for each morphine molecule. But if the concentration of morphine in the blood were three times the heroin concentration, the rate at which each crosses the blood-brain barrier would be the same. As a result of this, heroin is a *stronger* opiate than morphine, not a *faster* opiate.

Given this, it makes no sense that heroin cannot be prescribed in this country when it is identical to morphine in effect and yet is less toxic. The fact that Dilaudid can be prescribed is even more amazing since in addition to it being a more effective drug (three times as strong as heroin) there is less nausea associated with it — as a result of this, Dilaudid is particularly prized by opiate users.

The emphasis of this book is on the practical matters associated with heroin use. If you are interested in more information on brain chemistry and how heroin affects the brain, check out my book *The Little Book of Heroin.*

Heroin Compared to Other Drugs

There is little question that heroin is the drug with the most "street cred."[3] It has often been referred to as "the hardest drug." When I was growing up in and around the drug subculture, the conventional wisdom was that any drug was worth trying — except heroin. But these perceptions of heroin came from people who had never used the drug.

Drug "Hardness"

The attitudes about how "hard" a drug is, derive primarily from the method in which the drug is commonly administered. The order is as follows: eating (including drinking liquids), smoking, snorting, and injecting. This is not a fact that I base upon some

---

[3] "Street cred" is short for "street credibility." When one has "street cred," one has respect on the street — everybody knows that he isn't one who can be messed with.

elaborate sociological experiment;[4] it is based upon my keen observations over many years. But if you consider the recreational drugs, and how you think about them, you will see my point.

The eaten drugs are alcohol, caffeine, and even most prescription drugs — although their association with doctors and hospitals confuse matters. To most people, these are relatively safe; you don't generally have to worry about people finding out that you use them. Next we have the smoked drugs: mostly cigarettes and marijuana— even opium, although this is very rarely seen in the United States. (It's interesting what a big difference there is in the perceptions of opium and heroin even though they are pretty much the same thing.) These two categories seem relatively safe because they are familiar in our society: everyone eats and a lot of people smoke. To most people, the acts of eating and smoking do not imply that a drug is being ingested (although this is pretty much always the case with smoking).

Now we get to the category of hard drugs. For snorting, we have primarily cocaine and speed. Although these drugs are considered "hard" or "serious," they are perceived as a very significant step down from heroin — mostly because heroin is seen as always being injected. This is interesting in that both cocaine and speed are commonly injected and heroin is commonly smoked and snorted. In fact, opiate addicts only use heroin because of the laws and black market economics that result from them. Before there were laws against opiates, almost all addicts where addicted to opium — instead of heroin or morphine — which they administered mostly by drinking. Heroin addiction and the syringe are the result of laws, not of the powerful draw of heroin.

There are exceptions to this model, of course. LSD is eaten, for example. But overall, people do decide how dangerous a drug is on its administration route. My purpose in presenting this model of drug perceptions is to allow you to see that the people around you do not guide their thoughts about drugs on facts. This might be considered good by the drug warriors who think that it will keep

---

[4] Since developing this theory, I have found that Zinberg developed a similar theory in his studies of controlled drug use.

people from trying the "harder" drugs. In fact, while it will keep some people from using these drugs, it will also *cause* some people to use these drugs. I know that much of my interest in trying heroin originally was my belief that it was the hardest drug.

Drug Effects

So what does make a drug hard? This is an ill-posed question. Anyone who wants to think about drugs seriously should ask several different questions: 1. How profoundly does the drug affect thinking? 2. How much damage does the drug do to the body of the user? 3. How likely is the drug to cause misbehavior? 4. How bad is the withdrawal from the drug? Let me take on these questions one at a time.

Thinking Ability

How profoundly does a drug affect thinking? The drugs that have the greatest effect on cognitive ability are the psychedelics: marijuana and the LSD drugs. LSD is a powerful hallucinogen — most people won't question me here. But marijuana, that golden child of the illegal drug world which is almost legal? Yes. Very small doses of it have a profound effect on the cognitive abilities of the brain. One hit of middle-grade pot and I can barely talk. And this was true even when I was doing $200 of heroin per day.

Heroin does not have a great effect on the cognitive abilities of the brain. This is due to how morphine works. It is active mostly in the lower part of the brain, the brain stem. People do not think much differently on it than off of it. They do, however, think much more slowly.

Bodily Damage

How much damage does the drug do to the body of the user? There is no question that the drugs most damaging to the body are alcohol, speed, and cocaine. All of these drugs beat up the body excessively. Alcohol is a potent poison, which greatly taxes the liver and kidneys. It is also very effective at destroying brain tissue. The "white powders" destroy the kidneys even faster than alcohol destroys the liver.

Heroin can be damaging to the body in that it is possible to overdose on it and die. But most of the deaths that are attributed to "heroin overdose" are really due to other causes such as impurities and drug interactions (heroin and alcohol together, for example, is a prescription for death). The actual overdoses that occur are mostly due to the inconsistent quality of the drug. Otherwise, heroin is relatively gentle on the body. There are basically no long-term deleterious effects of heroin use.

Misbehavior

How likely is the drug to cause misbehavior? When it comes to the drug that causes most misbehavior, we're talking about everyone's favorite: alcohol. Alcohol makes people more aggressive and it has a high association with violent crimes. The good side of this is that it can act as a "social lubricator" by allowing normally shy people to be more outgoing. But this also makes people more prone to be belligerent and more likely to turn to violence.

Popularly, heroin is associated with crime like no other drug. There is no doubt that junkies do a lot of stealing. But this is not the result of the drug's effect. It is the effect of the laws and the fact that junkies will be very sick if they don't get their drugs. From their perspective it is medication — medication that costs a lot of money because it is illegal.[5] Heroin is not associated with violence at all; in fact, people under the influence of heroin are *less* likely to become violent than people under the influence of no drug. The effect of heroin on the user's personality is one of calming and sedation. A society of heroin addicts might well be a less productive one, but it would probably also be a more peaceful one.

Withdrawal

How bad is the withdrawal from the drug? Problems associated with physical addiction, namely withdrawal, are the worst for certain prescription drugs, in particular the barbiturates. Next comes

---

[5] If heroin were legal, even junkies with enormous habits would be spending at most a couple of dollars per day.

(again!) alcohol. In all cases, withdrawal can cause death. In rehab clinics, these kinds of addicts have to be monitored very carefully.

Withdrawal from any opiate is never pleasant (I will talk about this at length in Chapter Seven), but it is almost impossible to die from opiate withdrawal. When people do die from it, the cause is dehydration. With a little knowledge ("drink lots of water"), no heroin addict would ever die from withdrawal.

Seeing Heroin Objectively

All of this is not to say that heroin is a safe drug that should be fed to children. Heroin use can be dangerous. But heroin isn't *Satan in a Syringe*. When compared to other drugs, legal and illegal, it is relatively mild in effects and problems. We are a world of caffeine addicts who can't start the day without a fix. And withdrawal from the stuff can be miserable. If opium were legal it would be no better nor any worse.

I hope this discussion will cause you to be a little more reasonable about how you look at heroin. Don't start using it because you think it will be the most amazing experience of your life. It is just a drug, like many, many others. It has a good side and it has a bad side. You may like it or you may not. Regardless, you should base your decisions about heroin on facts, not rumor and propaganda.

Why Heroin Is Illegal

The whole opium family is in no sense worse than most legal drugs, but the legal status of drugs has very little to do with pharmacology, and a great deal to do with perceptions. From a medical standpoint, the nineteenth century saw a gradual move away from the use of opium and towards its isolated alkaloids such as morphine. It amazes people today, but at the turn of the century, heroin and aspirin were the two flagship products of Bayer. (See Figure 2.) Both were available throughout the United States without a prescription and society managed to move ahead without much of a problem. In fact, the politicians of that time were much more worried about opium than they were morphine or heroin. The reason was quite simple: hatred of Chinese immigrants.

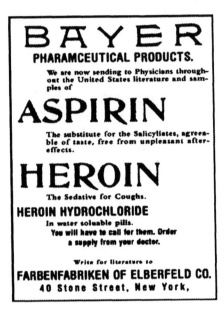

Figure 2

*At the turn of the century, heroin was sold over the counter,
right along with aspirin. This is an early Bayer Advertisement
featuring the company's two biggest products. The fact that heroin
was distributed in "water soluble pills" means that they could be
dissolved and injected, if the user wished.*

The public perception in the late 1800s was that the opium dens of the Chinese were acting as magnets to attract young women. This was a very xenophobic notion: the opium dens weren't bad because of the opium but rather because of the Chinese. But this isn't to say that the public concern wasn't warranted. Men, with their pounding testosterone, tended to like alcohol, but the more genteel women of the nineteenth century gravitated toward opium. At that time, opium was rarely even considered much of a vice since it did not cause anti-social behavior like alcohol.

As a result of this perception (fueled by latent hatred of Chinese people), various laws were passed limiting opium. San Francisco was the first city to pass a bill outlawing opium dens. California passed a law stating that Chinese people could not import opium into the state. The result of these and many similar laws was to make it harder and harder for people to use opium.

Of course, other than the fact that opium *was* more of a woman's drug, the public perceptions were wrong. The majority of the American opium users at that time were not even smoking opium, much less doing so in opium dens. They got high by drinking patent medicines, which contained high concentrations of opium.

The final blow to opium came in the form of the Harrison Narcotics Act which was really a tax act interpreted by law enforcement to outlaw these drugs. As *The Consumers Union Report on Licit and Illicit Drugs* notes, "It is unlikely that a single legislator realized in 1914 that the law Congress was passing would later be decreed a prohibition law."[6] The prohibition interpretation stemmed from the statement, "Nothing contained in this section shall apply ...to the dispensing or distribution of any of the aforesaid drugs to a patient by a physician... registered under this Act in the course of his professional practice only." This line was taken to mean that physicians could *only* prescribe these drugs to patients. Addicts were not patients since addiction was not seen as a disease at that time.[7] This interpretation is quite outrageous when

[6] Later in this century, it became commonplace for the federal government to use its ability to tax as a justification to prohibit. It is clear that the federal government has no constitutional right to prohibit drugs. These kind of constitutional gymnastics ("I can't prohibit, but I can tax, so I'll tax. Now that I'm taxing, I'll pretend that prohibiting is part of taxing!") are now commonplace and greatly limit the power of the United States Constitution.

[7] According to scientists, addiction is not a disease. However, the vast majority of people believe it is, mostly because of the acceptance of the dogma of *Alcoholics Anonymous* in the drug treatment community. This belief is shared by those in the criminal justice system, but for many reasons they continue to incarcerate rather than hospitalize "diseased" drug addicts.

one considers that the text of the law specifically allows for patent medicine manufacturers to be exempt from even licensing with the government as long as their medicines contained opiates below a set concentration. But a process had been underway for some time up until then to make opium harder and harder to acquire. This was similar to the current war being waged against cigarette smokers.

After the passage and interpretation of the Harrison Act, users had to just do without while addicts were forced to withdraw cold turkey or find an illegal or quasi-legal source. Most just gave up the drug, in part because they didn't even know they were addicted to anything (much like cigarette smokers and coffee drinkers a few decades ago).

Similar stories can be told about the legal status of most currently illegal drugs. In the name of a non-existent threat, which was bolstered by widespread racism against a particular group, laws were passed against various drugs. During the debate over the Harrison Act, there was explicit racism directed toward southern blacks who used cocaine. Marijuana became illegal because it was associated with Mexicans. Alcohol is legal, not because it is safe (as I've noted above, it *isn't* safe), but because it is the drug of Europeans — that is, "us" not "them."

The point of this discussion is that the legal status of heroin is not based upon the effects of the drug itself. Rather, it is based on perceptions of the drug and its users. A funny aspect of this is that stereotypes of the Chinese opium smoker spawned the modern heroin addict, who now has his own stereotypes.

Heroin Can Be Used Safely

I had a dream recently:

> *There were these bleachers set up on the beach. People were sitting in them like they were at Sea World waiting for the water skiing show to start. In the bleachers was a diving board and people, mostly young men, were getting on to this board and diving into the ocean. I wasn't in the bleach-*

*ers, I was walking along the beach. From there, I watched
diver after diver land, not in the water, but on to the beach.
Their twisted and battered remains littered the sand.*

*I knew what was happening. The night before I had no-
ticed some suspicious people working on the diving board.
Whatever they did made the board less springy and so the
divers didn't have enough energy to make it to the safety of
the water. No one in the bleachers, including those lining
up to dive, seemed aware of what was happening to the divers. Or maybe they just didn't care.*

*I made my way through the bleachers and to the board
where I alerted the divers to the problem: the back of the
board was no longer secured to the bleachers and so the divers were falling short. They all re-attached the back of the
board and began diving again. I watched several people as
they dived. Now they would bounce upward, begin to fall
and then soar off like the children in Peter Pan, eventually
landing safely in the water. It was magical and I walked
away feeling a lot better.*

A friend of mine had to explain the dream to me: the divers are
the heroin users, the people in the bleachers are society, and the
repair of the board is this book, or at least what I would like this
book to be. Using heroin will always be dangerous, but it doesn't
need to be as dangerous as it is. However, what I really like about
this dream is that the divers fix the board — all I do is point out
the problem. This is very true: all I can do is provide information.
It is up to each user to take the steps necessary to stay healthy and
safe.

Heroin is not a drug that one can use without profound consequences. If your straight friends and family find out about your
use, they will not think of you as a recreational drug user; they will
think of you as a junkie with all of the negative connotations that
the word conjures. This is due to the fact that most people think it
is impossible to use heroin without becoming an addict. I have lost
friends just because they found out that I used heroin. Under-
standably, many people worry that heroin has such an overpow-

ering effect that it will cause you to harm them in some way (usually monetarily).

It's easy to become a drunk. All you have to do is walk down to the liquor store. But becoming a junkie takes a little work, while becoming a non-addicted user (a "chipper") takes a lot more. The primary concern of this book is to keep users in the chipping category and out of the junkie category. I know from experience that being a chipper can be a lot of fun because heroin is part of your life. But being a junkie sucks, because heroin *is* your life.

Chapter Two
Acquisition

Let's get one thing straight: I cannot tell you on which street corner to stand to score heroin, although in some cities I could. In San Francisco, for example, the heroin dealers do congregate on particular street corners and if you ask for syringes (which are also illegal) they'll send you to another street corner where all of the "outfit" dealers congregate. Nor can I give you a collection of pager numbers even though I do know about 20, spanning the cities of Seattle, Portland, San Francisco, and New York.[1] But I *can* give you the information necessary to know which street corners of major cities to stand on and how to acquire 20 pager numbers.

Everything that I talk about in this book is illegal, but this is the chapter that is most likely to get you into trouble. People are very rarely arrested while using. It is the act of scoring that most exposes you to detection by law enforcement. But remember the positive side: you can die from using heroin; acquiring it is only likely to get you arrested.

---

[1] Actually, it is unlikely that any of the pager numbers I know are still active. There is a high turnover rate with dealer pager numbers and it has been a long time since I have been actively involved in the heroin scene.

Heroin Distribution

Despite what some (mostly fear-mongering drug warriors) would have you believe, scoring heroin is not easy. It isn't handed out like candy in schoolyards and it isn't "pushed" on anyone. I've mentioned how much the heroin user has to lose if detected by law enforcement; the situation is far worse for the heroin dealer. As a result of this, most dealers are very careful. When acquiring a new connection it is quite common for a user to be asked to show track marks. This is a good example of the care that drug dealers take to avoid legal problems. It also shows just how ludicrous is the idea of the drug "pusher."

The secret to acquiring heroin successfully is knowledge — knowledge that you will find in this chapter and knowledge of your local heroin community. If you lack this knowledge you will get ripped off or arrested, neither of which is pleasant.

Pretty much all of the world's heroin used to be funneled through France, where opium from Asia was processed into heroin for shipment to users throughout Europe and the United States. Increased law enforcement efforts in France caused Mexico to become an important processing location. Most recently, Colombia has become a major source of heroin. (See Figure 3.) This is one reason why it is impossible for law enforcement to curtail the flow of heroin (or any product that people want to buy): There are always many people eager to fill any hole in this lucrative marketplace.[2]

But even when law enforcement (or poor opium crops or any number of other things) does manage to make a dent in the short-term importation of heroin into this country, the result is only more pain and suffering on the part of users. The dealers still make the same amount of money. This is due to the fact that the heroin

---

[2] Ironically, the successful law enforcement effort to crush the French Connection resulted in major long-term benefits to heroin users. The disruption of this supply of heroin caused the Italian Mafia to lose its near monopoly in the distribution process. As a result, competition flourished, causing prices to fall and purity to rise. Go, cops!

sold on the street is not the chemical heroin — diacetyl morphine. The heroin on the street is a bunch of filler that is combined with the chemical heroin. If less chemical heroin comes into the country, then the street heroin will simply contain less diacetyl morphine.

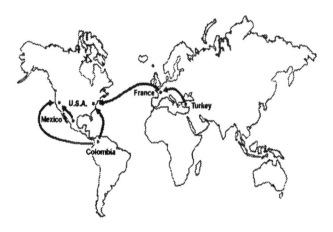

Figure 3
There are three primary routes for heroin transported into the United States. Opium from Turkey is processed into heroin in France before being transported to the U.S. It is also transported directly from Mexico and Colombia.

This explains why heroin quality can vary from day to day. There are, however, broad trends in heroin quality. Heroin is stronger today than it has ever been. Average street heroin is about 50% pure, but it can be found as pure as 80%. Heroin quality was at its worst around 1970 when the purity was averaging 3%. At that time junkies who were arrested and put in jail were often surprised to find that they weren't really sick. A $100 per day habit today would have been a $2000 per day habit in 1970.

Today, on the east coast of the U.S., heroin is distributed as a white powder. This is the heroin that is still coming out of France and increasingly, Colombia. White powder heroin looks about the same regardless of what it is cut with. As a result of this, users used to "taste" the heroin; a bitter taste indicated it was relatively pure. Heroin, however has been cut by quinine — which also has a bitter taste — for a very long time and so the practice is really not engaged in anymore.

On the west coast, heroin is distributed as a black substance known as "black tar," which can take on a number of forms depending upon what adulterants are used in it. When cut with sugar it tends to be crystalline. When cut with coffee, it can be smelled clearly. At its most pure, it is somewhat gooey and black.

Many users believe that white powder heroin is purer than black tar heroin. This is not the case. The truth is in the using. One thing that I have noticed is that white powder heroin is more variable in its purity than black tar. This may be because my black tar connections were better than my white powder connections, but it seems more likely that it is due to the fact that the black tar heroin was coming from a closer source (Mexico) and so its distribution chain was more set. The point is that the form heroin comes in is indicative of where it comes from and nothing more.

During the importation process, heroin goes through many hands, which "step on" (adulterate) it. In the early 1970s, for example, there was a whole sequence of distributors — each of whom cut the product — resulting in the very low purity of that time. The high purity levels today indicate that the distribution chain is much shorter.

Local areas will have differences in quality and price, but I have found that you get what you pay for. Heroin that goes for $150 a gram is usually very pure. Heroin that goes for $40 a gram is usually poor. This local pricing is the result of an informal agreement between sellers and users. If the users want to buy a gram of heroin for $40, the local sellers will provide it, but only after they cut it a great deal.

Prices in a particular area are usually very stable. If it was $40 a gram last year, it is still $40 a gram. Quality is what is unstable. This instability does not come about because your local dealer is cutting the heroin more or less, depending upon how the mood hits him. It is the result of the fact that all the heroin coming into your area is of a lower quality.

Acquirers

Most people do not wake up one morning and think, "Wow, it'd be nice to try heroin; I think I'll go get a book on it." If you're reading this book you've probably already tried it. This puts you in a very good position to score it, because you at least know someone who knows someone who can get it.

Let me tell you how it worked for me. My girlfriend knew some people who used heroin. I was interested in trying it, having long had a great love of codeine, and so she had them score us a $10 bag. This bag lasted us a good six months[3] by which time we had lost track of our connection. However, we managed to get another connection — a local bartender was friends with a kid who would score on the street for a small amount of the score. We started hanging out as a group. It turned out that the kid's roommate was really into heroin and was having the kid score for her. But she, like us, was getting tired of the poor quality of the street heroin as well as getting ripped off in more overt ways (one time she bought a balloon filled with a pebble). She badgered people she knew until she finally got a pager number. So started the salad days.

For a good three months she became our connection selling us $20 bags for $30. I was only too happy to pay the extra amount — I felt that it insulated me further from law enforcement. The quality was excellent and we never got burned. The problem was that our connection also had a heroin problem. She was doing up to $100 a day which she supported by dealing, stealing from work, and eliminating her savings. Eventually she turned against heroin, joined NA, and would have nothing to do with us.

In the meantime, I had set up another connection. A user friend had left town for a job in New York where he quickly became addicted to heroin despite a decade and a half of chipping (see Chapter Six). As such, he had four very steady sources of heroin.

---

[3] Heroin is a very cheap drug if you do not do it very often.

So I set up for him to score heroin with my money, take half of it for himself, and mail the rest back to me. Expensive, but convenient: heroin right to your door![4]

After a few months of this, I went on a vacation to New York. When I got there I found out that my friend had decided to get clean. He gave me the pager numbers for all of his dealers, however. I managed to work out a deal with one of these connections, who I then asked if he would be willing to do the mail-order thing with me. He asked why I didn't do this with my friend and I told him that he was now clean. At that point the dealer became pensive and said, "I just got a call from him."

It's interesting to note that this was the first time that I had any contact with a real dealer. Up to this point, I had been scoring entirely from people who knew dealers. Overall, this was a good development because I was paying a lot less for the heroin I was using and my risk had not gone up very much as a result — well, my risk from law enforcement had not changed; my risk from addiction had certainly increased.

I think you can see from this twisted story that the path to an initial connection can be tortuous. But this story illustrates the best way to get a connection. The friends that I was getting heroin from are what are known as "acquirers." They are people who buy drugs at street prices and sell them (either for a monetary profit or for a cut or even for free) to friends who do not want to take the risk of scoring on the street and do not have a regular connection. The upside to dealing with an acquirer is that they do insulate you from law enforcement and they are relatively easy to find. The downside is that you pay more for the drugs than you normally would. For a chipper this is usually no big deal, but for a junkie it is completely unacceptable. In fact, junkies almost always do a little acquiring.

---

[4] I don't recommend this. Small packages do tend to get overlooked by the post office, but people are caught doing this. It is much more likely that one would get caught with a drug that smells, such as marijuana (as Bob "Gilligan" Denver did recently), but this opens up a user to more risk than when dealing with an acquirer directly.

Heroin Subculture

Before talking about finding an acquirer, I need to deal with the heroin subculture a little (I will come back to this in more detail in Chapter Six). You can think of the heroin subculture as a series of concentric circles. In the centermost circles are the dealers. Huddled very closely around this circle is the junkie circle. People in this group generally have many pager numbers and can score easily on the street. They may meet with a dealer a few times in a day. Casual chippers are unlikely to have contact with people in this category because junkies are so immersed in heroin that they are almost invisible — mostly because they are working too hard supporting their habits.

Outside this circle you find unsuccessful junkies and serious chippers. These people may have a pager number, but are more likely to score on the street or deal with an acquirer (someone in the junkie circle). Further out, you have people who have tried heroin once or twice and ex-addicts. These people may still know chippers or junkies or even dealers. Then again, they may not.

In the final circle are all of the straight people. These people cannot help you. Worse than this: they can be dangerous. In general, straight people think that heroin is *Satan in a Syringe* and they may turn you into the authorities "for your own good." For this reason, you need to be very careful as you make your way around and into the heroin subculture.

Finding an Acquirer

Finding an acquirer, if you don't already know one, is relatively easy, but it can take a little time. The key is to make new friends — friends who are at least on the periphery of the heroin subculture.

Pick a Bar

Start by checking bars. You don't want a dance club. You want a bar where people talk. Your best bet is a neighborhood bar in a city. It should be at least a little bit seedy and should be frequented by a fair cross-section of people. It is important that you don't pick an inbred bar — one where all the people are all the same — such as a yuppie bar. The bar should offer a variety of people from which to choose.

It is best to target a single promising bar because in doing so you will become known by the employees and the regulars and this will make you seem safer. Remember that no one knows what you are doing there — they just think that you are socializing. In fact, this is what you should be doing. If you don't get into the scene at the bar you probably won't make any friends and therefore won't find an acquirer. You need to enjoy this process — if you don't, you need to find a different process (check out the discussion of prostitutes below).

Search as a Couple

It will help your search if you are a part of a mixed gender couple. For one thing, this makes you less suspicious. Police rarely go to the extremes necessary to put a woman and a man undercover. In addition, people don't think of women as being cops (though they are, of course). A woman alone is a target for sexual advances — this may help in the search but it may complicate matters in a way you do not want. Being part of a couple also has the advantage; that as a pair it is easier to overcome shyness and start conversations with strangers. Gender doesn't matter in this case. Of course, if you are part of a same-sex couple, find a gay or lesbian bar.

Be a Good Listener

People sitting alone in bars are usually interested in talking, especially if the other person is a good listener and not someone who wants to dominate the conversation. You must be a good listener because you are trying to get information. In the long run, the information you are trying to get is whether this person can get you heroin. But heroin is not a subject you should even talk about until you know your target reasonably well. At first you should just be trying to make friends. You need to find out if the person you're talking to is someone you want to know. There are plenty of people who can get you heroin who you don't want to deal with. So try to make friends.

Fit In

You want to come off a certain way during this process. Dress the way most of the people who hang out at the bar dress. You must drink alcohol — no one trusts a sober person when they are drinking. Try to come off a little "curved:" not straight, but not a drug addict. You can reasonably talk about your adventures while drinking: for example, your love of pot. If you think you can pull it off, you can even talk about that time you *tried* opium while traveling in Asia. None of these things is likely to cause a stir in a bar.

Be Generous

Spread a little money around — buy drinks, but don't be obnoxious. Some people love it when people buy them drinks but others find it insulting. Start by "buying a round." The implication is that someone else will pick up the next. From there you can try to buy a second round or buy a round the next time you're together. In this way, you can feel people out. Spending money on friends will make them want to be around you more (I realize this is cynical, but that's life). Be careful, however. If you throw around too much money you will make people nervous (the very people who can help you) or set yourself up as a mark.

Investigate Good Prospects

If you find someone who looks like a good candidate, check him out. At this point in your relationship you should know where he works. Stop by unannounced some time and see if he really is what he claims to be. You can make up some excuse, such as you just got a bonus and you wanted to take him to lunch. If you think this would be seen as invasive, you could send someone else to snoop around or do so yourself, but very carefully.

The Big Question

Bringing up the subject of heroin must be done delicately. If you've found a candidate, chances are that he has already mentioned past involvement with the drug. If there is no obvious opportunity you can gently push a conversation about any illegal drug in that direction. It's easier to say, "Have you ever tried opium?" than it is to say, "Have you ever tried heroin?" But even this is unnecessary. Almost everyone has been given Vicodin at one time or another. You can move from there.

When you finally do get to The Big Question, be gentle. Don't say, "Do you know where to get heroin?" Instead say, "I've always been really curious about heroin, but I wouldn't want to inject anything." Adding the disclaimer about injecting serves two purposes. First, it emphasizes that you aren't a "hard" drug user — you don't inject and wouldn't even consider it. Second, it is an invitation to your potential acquirer to correct you: "It doesn't have to be injected." If you get that response, you're home free. The conversation will naturally go toward a discussion of heroin where, at some point, you can add, "I wouldn't know how to go about scoring it."

Certainly, this is a conversation that you couldn't very well have the first time you meet someone. Even if your target was this open with you, you would be foolish to reveal so much about yourself. Especially these days of the Drug War, where great time and expense is given to catching users. You can't tell who is a cop and who isn't. Check people out before you trust them.

The same goes for the acquirer. There is nothing that would stop a cop from reading this book and using the information to catch "dealers."[5] The acquirer must be very careful about the people he deals with. Familiarity does not make a person safe. Information is the only thing that makes a person trustworthy.

Dealing with an Acquirer

Even after you find an acquirer, there may be many problems. If he has a connection, it will often take several days to track down his connection. If he is scoring on the street, he may get burned. Time and money are the price you pay for the knowledge you gain in finding an acquirer. But having an acquirer is a door into the heroin subculture, and it is a fairly safe door. You open up a whole new world while keeping your feet firmly planted in the straight world. How long you keep your feet so planted is up to you. The looser your feet become, the more danger you expose yourself to.

---

[5] From a legal standpoint, acquirers are dealers even if they do not profit from the exchange.

Scoring on the Street

Many users love scoring on the street. It is exciting, challenging, and dangerous. Regardless of a user's feelings about scoring on the street, however, sometimes it is the only way to acquire heroin.

Of course, scoring on the street successfully is a matter of knowledge, but it is also about attitude. You have got to be able to walk the walk and talk the talk. Otherwise, the only people who will be willing to deal with you are cops and thieves. When you are on the street, you need to look like a junkie. But in doing so, you walk a razor's edge: you want the dealers to think that you're a junkie, but not the police. This is where knowledge is critical. You need to be able to spot a dealer, make the deal quickly, and leave.

Looking Like a Junkie

Appearing to be a junkie was always easy for me. Long before I had ever tried heroin I was accused of being a junkie because I was so skinny and, since I was usually cold, I always wore long sleeves. If you are a large person, it will be a little harder. For one thing, police forces hire big people but they don't hire little wisps of men like me. Junkies come in all shapes and sizes, but there are generalities.

The common image of a junkie is summed up well in a 1962 Supreme Court decision: "A confirmed drug addict is ...one of the walking dead." This may be true when the drug is alcohol; certainly, the homeless drunks give this impression. When the drug is heroin, this is certainly *not* the case. A junkie is generally the guy walking down the street at a near run with his eyes darting in every direction. Being a junkie is one of the most challenging occupations imaginable. He can't afford to be "out of it." When on the street, a junkie is about the most alert person you'll see.

Whether a junkie has a regular job or scrapes and steals to get by, he doesn't have a lot of time. He is busy doing whatever he must to get money. For the unemployed (in a traditional sense) junkie the situation is almost unimaginable for a straight person.

Think what it would be like to wake up every morning with no money, no job, no family to turn to, and know that you had to get, say $100. What would you do? If you haven't lived it you probably don't know. Most junkies who do it can't even tell you. They just get out onto the street and find the money anyway they can think of. And some of the ways they think of are quite ingenious. Being a junkie (especially one with a large habit and no traditional job) is extremely challenging and active.

In scoring on the street you want to look like a junkie. If you walk down the street looking like the Supreme Court's idea of what a junkie is, you won't ever find heroin. While trolling for heroin you should look alert and walk at a fairly brisk pace. But don't walk too fast or the dealers will not have enough time to react to you and you want to limit the number of times you walk by the same location.

You also won't find heroin if you're dressed in a tuxedo. Unless it is hot, junkies tend to layer clothing. Even when it is hot, they will tend to wear long sleeves. But other than this they don't really look any different than anyone else that you will see on the street.

Approaching a Dealer

Except under unusual circumstances it is best to not approach dealers. If you see someone who looks promising, walk by him and try to catch his eye. If he is a dealer, he wants to sell to you as long as he feels confident you are a user and not a cop. If at first you don't succeed, walk by a few more times so that he'll get the idea. In doing so try to look a little lost so that other (straight) people don't figure out what you are up to.

In many areas, there are "hooks" who lead users to dealers. You need to be careful with these people. To start, you will get a worse deal from the dealer proper because the hook gets a cut. In addition, hooks will often foist themselves on you and refuse to go away until you pay them for their "help." I have had some very bad experiences with hooks that amounted to nothing short of robbery. In one case a large black man insisted that I give him a bag of heroin because I would not pay attention to him and use the dealer he was trying to get me to use (I had already found another dealer by the time I noticed this hook). This confrontation ended with him grabbing me around the neck and choking me until I gave him a bag of heroin. Unless you really need a hook, avoid them. Make a point of not making eye contact with any people other than those you think are dealers; hooks often take eye contact as meaning they own you.

Location

A key element in scoring is location. In any city there will be locations where drugs simply are not sold. There will also be locations where drugs are sold, but heroin is not sold. A good example of this is Washington Square Park in New York. Although it is possible to score heroin there, it is really the place to score marijuana. The locations where you will find drugs are those where there are a lot of people hanging out on the street. In Portland, the bus mall is such a place. But even better is the downtown part of Burnside Boulevard. The reason for this is that a lot of homeless and unemployed people hang out there basically doing nothing. This is a good place for dealers to hang out without being noticed.

For whatever reasons, heroin is mostly a white person's drug these days. There are certainly a lot of black junkies, and Hispanic and even Native American, but on the whole one finds Anglo Saxons to be the primary partakers. If you find a neighborhood that is primarily black you probably won't find heroin — you'll most likely find crack. So stick to mixed neighborhoods with large white populations.

If you just don't know where to look for heroin, go to the library. Your local newspaper will no doubt have run some articles on the "heroin problem" in your community. These articles usually contain quite a bit of information about the heroin scene — in particular they will tell you where it is located. But remember that the newspaper got its information from the police so the area that you go to will be reasonably well monitored by the police.

Before you go out and try to score, go to a likely spot and hang out. Just watch what is going on. Try to figure out who the dealers are, who the junkies are, who the police are likely to bother. An hour or two spent making such observations can be highly educational. But don't expect to see an actual drug deal go down. The dealers and the buyers are usually a little more discreet than that. But many other things will be revealing.

Prostitutes

There are other options in scoring on the street. One is to find a prostitute. Prostitution is not as big a crime as heroin use. In most places, the act of propositioning someone is only a misdemeanor. As a result, if you proposition a cop you will not have as many problems as if you try to score heroin from a cop. So if you negotiate a sex deal and don't end up arrested or ticketed, you know you aren't dealing with a cop.

There are two reasons why prostitutes can help you. First, they understand the streets and know what is going on. Second, many of them are junkies. For money or drugs they can usually acquire what you want. Of course, just like with any other acquirer, the price you pay is extra money. But one aspect of dealing with a prostitute is that you will usually get more than just the drugs — and I don't mean sex. Hanging out with her (or him) will teach you a lot about how the scene works.

Call-Back Phones

The fact that most cities have few "call back" phones also offers you a scoring opportunity. You can hang out near such a phone and before too long a junkie will probably use the phone to page his dealer. But you must be careful. Cops sometimes monitor such phones so that they can follow the caller to the dealer and make an arrest. As a result, you need to approach the caller with care or you will frighten him away.

Let me leave this subject with a caution. Under most circumstances, never give money to someone who will go away and get the drugs. This is just a set up to getting ripped off. Similarly, don't give someone money to "hold." This is usually put forward as, "you've got to give me the money; they don't trust you." Just say no and continue to say no. If it isn't a set up they will give in eventually. The main exception is when you are dealing with prostitutes. Generally they won't rip you off because they have too high a profile and they are afraid of getting hurt. But even with them, it is best to dangle a carrot. Tell them that if the dope is okay you will buy more and split it. If the prostitute is straight with you, make good on your deal.

Connections

Having a regular connection will make your life better and safer. Since you know who you are dealing with, you don't have to worry about being ripped off. Also, you can arrange to meet in places that are safer instead of known drug selling areas.

Street

If you are scoring on the street, it is just a matter of time before you get a regular connection. Most of the time, it is no problem to simply ask a dealer if he has a pager or cell phone number. If you score from the same dealer a few times, he is likely to bring it up himself. The truth of the matter is that if you are not a cop, it's safer for both of you to communicate via telephone. Dealers are also more willing to give out this information when business is slow. I've been offered a lot more pager numbers at 2:00 a.m. than I have 10:00 p.m. This may be because people buying drugs in the wee hours of the morning appear to be more serious about their drug use.

Acquirers

Getting a connection through an acquirer is more difficult. Remember that you owe your acquirer because he is taking a risk for you. He will probably be annoyed if you try to bypass him. As a result you should bide your time. Eventually, he may get bored with dealing with you or he may decide he doesn't want to be involved with heroin anymore. This is the time to ask him for an introduction to his connection. Other than the fact that he may consider this a hassle, there should not be a problem. He can vouch for the fact that you are a user and that you have been for some time. This should be enough to convince his connection to do business with you.

Using a Connection

At first, the process of scoring from a connection is a bit of a pain — worse than scoring on the street or through an acquirer. In the long-run, it is better. But there are usually a few problems that must be overcome before using your connection works well.

Pay Phones

Under most circumstances, you will page your dealer. Paging alone can introduce all kinds of obstacles for you if you don't live locally, because you will have to use a pay phone. Most pay phones don't accept incoming calls these days. As a result it may take some time to find a pay phone that does. Pay phones are usually posted as not taking incoming calls, but some pay phones are not posted and still don't take incoming calls. The best way to check is to use the phone to call yourself (the pay phone you are using). If you get a busy signal, the phone takes incoming calls. But this does not assure that the ringer on the phone works. This is usually not a problem but if you're worried, call from a nearby phone, but remember that most pay phones have rather quiet ringers and this may require that you have a partner stand near the phone you're testing.

Even if a pay phone does take incoming calls, it may not have the phone number posted. To find out the number, call the operator and request the pay phone's number. They are generally glad to give the information. A lot of straight people need to use pagers for perfectly lawful reasons, so don't worry that it will seem odd. Once you get the number, write it down on the phone book or the phone itself. This will be helpful to you and others in the future.

Once your dealer calls you back, he will have you meet him somewhere on the street at some time. Don't be surprised if your dealer says, "Fifteen minutes," and you end up waiting an hour. Eventually he will arrive. If he speaks English, you are in luck. Try to get him to have you wait somewhere that doesn't draw attention. My favorite place is in front of a movie theater because people commonly wait for friends there. Make a general suggestion along these lines. Let him decide on the specific location — drug dealers are always worried that they are being set up, even by longtime customers.

Meeting at Home

Eventually, it is nice to have your dealer come to your home. It is safer and more pleasant than hanging out on street corners. This is not something most dealers feel very comfortable about doing until they have known you for a while. It is not just fear of police that causes this. In your own home, they can be ripped off or worse. Wait awhile before you bring it up and expect that you will have to bring it up several times before a dealer will agree.

Once you have a dealer coming to your home, be careful about the frequency with which he comes and how long he stays. If you have a dealer coming to your house every day, and staying only a minute, your neighbors may notice and call the police. Try to get your dealers to stay awhile. In Portland, we did this by turning our television on to the Hispanic station. After awhile it was hard to get the dealers to leave. As a chipper, it isn't hard to limit the number of visits. As a junkie, you have little choice. In this case, get your dealers to meet you away from your home as much as possible. Save the home visits for when you're sick or the weather is really bad.

A Caution

Working your way to a connection can be very exciting. You open up a whole world to yourself. But you also open yourself up to a lot of danger. The most obvious danger is from law enforcement. There are other dangers, however. The people you deal with have already taken a big step outside of law-abiding society. This isn't to say that they don't maintain their own ethics: they do. But they aren't necessarily *your* ethics. Even though I've never met a junkie I would consider evil, junkies are often desperate and desperation can make them do bad things. I know I've done rotten things that wouldn't even occur to me now. You must be careful about the people with whom you are dealing — always.

A bigger concern is addiction. If you are going to become addicted it will most likely happen right after you get a regular connection. When one is scraping just to find heroin, it is hard to do it often enough to get strung out. But when you don't have to worry so much about getting it, you can do it every day — and that is how you get addicted. (See Chapter Four for information on how to avoid addiction.) But remember: a lot of people know how to avoid addiction, but get addicted anyway.

Chapter Three
Ingestion

Probably the most important decision that you will make as a heroin user is how to administer the drug. In this chapter I will discuss the primary means of administering it. There are many options and all of them have advantages and disadvantages, so it is in your best interest to study this chapter carefully. As with all aspects of heroin, there are many myths associated with its ingestion, which can cause you great harm. This is the most important chapter in this book.

This chapter begins with an overview of the primary techniques and ends with specific instructions and procedures for each technique. In addition to this discussion, you should read Chapter Four for information on the risks associated with the ingestion of heroin. I cannot stress enough the importance of this information. This is literally a matter of life and death.

Overview

There are three primary means of ingesting heroin: injection, smoking, and snorting. Each of these techniques has variations, particularly injection. There are other methods, but these are rarely used — methods such as the use of anal suppositories made somewhat famous in the film *Trainspotting*. For most users these

other techniques are of limited interest. As a result, I will only discuss these three methods.

Injection

There are three ways of injecting any drug: intravenously, intramuscularly, and subcutaneously. These are commonly referred
to as "mainlining," "muscling," and "skin popping." Mainlining is
as different from the other two methods as it is from snorting. As a
result they must be considered separately.

Intravenous

Mainlining is the method that most people associate with junkies. It is the most direct way of administering heroin (although not
the fastest). If you've ever given blood, then you know the process: you tie off your arm so that your veins stand out. Then you
stick the sharp end of the syringe into a promising vein. At this
point the contents of the syringe are flushed into the bloodstream.
The heroin travels through the veins to the liver and heart; from
there it finally goes to the brain. The most important aspect of this
method is that a minimum quantity of the heroin is destroyed
before reaching the brain.

There are other advantages to mainlining. Almost as important
as its lack of waste (and most important to many users), is that the
heroin is delivered to the brain in a concentrated form for a strong
rush. For many, there is an added advantage in that they enjoy the
injection process itself. This may seem odd, but one of the appeals
of any drug is the set of rituals that surround it, and for heroin,
mainlining has an unmistakable ritual element. When I quit using
heroin I injected water for a while just because I missed the injection process. I wasn't alone — other ex-users have told me they
have done the same thing.

The lack of waste associated with mainlining cannot be under-
estimated in its appeal. Heroin users have found that their intake
was reduced by a factor of four when they switched from smoking
heroin to shooting it (my experience indicates that shooting is
about twice as effective as smoking when one smokes using the
efficient procedure discussed later in this chapter). For addicts,

this is a huge savings, which is why addicts will generally switch to slamming dope if they are not already.

For the casual user, the appeal of mainlining is mostly in the rush they get from the process. I have known many non-addicts who mainline, so it should not be considered simply the method of junkies. But because of its many drawbacks and, for them, minor advantages, chippers often avoid mainlining.

The main disadvantage of mainlining heroin is that it is more prone to cause an overdose, and care must always be taken. The use of needles also requires a greater commitment to medical cleanliness because of the danger of various diseases, some of which can kill you (this is not an overstatement). Finally, mainlining is rather difficult to do. It takes time to learn and it is definitely not for the squeamish. Plus, if you do it wrong, even with medical cleanliness, you can hurt yourself.

Intramuscular

Intramuscular injection is easy to do — that is its main advantage, even though it requires as much attention to cleanliness as mainlining. This method is often used by addicts who can no longer find a vein in which to inject. This method has more disadvantages than advantages. The most important disadvantage is that this is an indirect ingestion technique. Much of the heroin is destroyed before getting to the brain and there is no rush associated with it. More important to some users, injecting into a muscle is somewhat painful. Other methods are preferable to intramuscular injections.

Subcutaneous

The idea with skin popping is to inject the drug just under the skin, where there are many small blood vessels, which will take up the drug and get you high. It has the disadvantages of intramuscular injection although it is somewhat less wasteful. It has the added disadvantage that it requires some technique although it can be much easier than mainlining. During injection, a bubble of heroin develops under the skin, which, while not painful, can be frightening. The skin can puff up to a startling extent. This will dissipate over the course of 10 to 15 minutes. This technique is also commonly used by junkies with bad veins. Once again, it is not a technique I recommend.

Snorting

The scientific literature refers to the ingestion of drugs through the nasal mucous membranes as "sniffing" and "inhalation." If you have a straw stuck up your nose doing your best imitation of a Hoover vacuum on a bunch of white powder piled into neat little lines, you would normally say you were snorting.

Snorting is much more common where heroin is distributed as a powder, because it is easy to ingest and has an obvious analogy to using cocaine, which is familiar to most users. Snorting it can be done with black tar as well but it is harder to do and takes more preparation. Snorting has many advantages: it is fairly easy to do and for most users it does not seem at all foreign or dangerous because of experience with other drugs; it is relatively safe in terms of dangers from impurities; it does not require specialized equipment; and it is not particularly prone to spreading disease.

As is the case with most procedures, the upside and the downside of snorting heroin is the same. Snorting is relatively safe because the path taken to the brain acts as a buffer filtering out impurities. Just the same, your body also filters out the heroin. So even though you can't see the wasted heroin as you can when it is smoked, there is still a lot of wasted heroin.

Another bad aspect of snorting heroin is that it is hard to gauge how high you are when doing it. Unlike mainlining and smoking, there is a significant period of time between snorting the heroin and actually feeling its effects. This means that an over-eager snorter may well get much more high than he had planned. This can bring on nausea, other common side-effects of heroin, and even overdose.

When using brown tar heroin, the procedure for snorting is much more involved. The heroin must be cooked and dissolved in water just as if it were to be injected. As a result, one of the advantages of snorting disappears — namely, the ease of use. However, it does have the advantage in that the cooking process reduces the risk of disease.

Smoking

Smoking is naturally associated with brown tar heroin in much the same way that snorting is associated with white powder. Because of its obvious wasteful nature (the heroin just goes up in smoke), smoking is often derided by other users. Although this method can be highly wasteful, it depends entirely upon technique; the obvious "up in smoke" aspect of waste can be entirely eliminated, as is discussed below.

A little known fact of drug taking is that smoking is the fastest way to administer a drug. This goes against most notions of drug use because it would seem that pumping a drug directly into your vein is the most direct means of administration. But getting the drug into your circulatory system will not get you high — you have to get it to your brain. Drugs taken intravenously take a circuitous path to the brain: through the veins, to the liver, and then to the heart before delivery to the brain. Smoking causes a drug to be absorbed by the lungs where it is transferred to the arteries and delivered directly to the brain. But don't be misled: mainlining will get you higher than smoking. The fact is that it takes time to smoke heroin; you can't smoke a gram all at once. Smoking will give you a rush, but it is not the same as slamming.

In general, smoking is safe: it will get you higher than any method other than mainlining, it's easy to do and doesn't require any special or illegal equipment. The downside of smoking is varied. Smoking is the middle-ground procedure for heroin administration. Since it uses a direct pathway to your brain, it is inherently less safe than less direct means like snorting. It ranges from somewhat wasteful to very wasteful, depending upon your technique. It is fairly difficult to smoke heroin alone, which is both good and bad: it makes smoking a good method for social drug use.

Other Methods

There are plenty of other ways to ingest heroin. Most probably won't interest you unless you have special interests. The methods already mentioned are the most promising. You must remember that users have been working on the problem of ingestion for decades and it isn't likely that you'll revolutionize the drug-taking world. But if it makes you happy, go ahead and rub heroin on open sores. The truth is, you never know. One time, I tried using heroin with DMSO on my skin. I used a large amount of heroin just to make sure that even if the effect were small I would still feel it. The result was that I didn't feel anything — the DMSO did, however, cause my arm to break out in about a hundred pinhead-sized bumps. Such are the trials of the experimental drug user.

In the following sections I am going to discuss the process of administering heroin. This is done in a step-by-step manner so that the procedures are very clear. Even if you are an experienced user, it is a good idea to pay very close attention to these sections and not just skim through them. The details of each procedure are often critical and can make the difference (in some cases) between life and death. Heroin is a dangerous drug, but users are much more likely to get hurt by the process of administration rather than by heroin itself.

Injection

The process of injecting heroin can be broadly subdivided into two parts. First, the solution is prepared and put into a syringe (See Figure 4). Second, the contents of the syringe are flushed into the body: either a muscle, vein, or blood vessel layer. The idea behind good shooting technique is to insure that the syringe remains clean until it enters the body and that it enters the right place in the body.

Hygiene

If you do nothing else, you will greatly decrease your problems getting high on heroin by simply using new needles every time you shoot up. This sounds easy enough, but yet even though all the time I was using heroin I lived in a state in which needles are perfectly legal — costing roughly a quarter apiece — I had never met a user who utilized clean needles for every administration. In many cases, users were unaware that syringes were legal, but still continued as before even after they were educated on the matter.

With all of the problems associated with using heroin, many users find the acquisition of syringes a hassle that they can easily neglect. This is unfortunate, since dirty syringes can kill a user in more than one way.

Another easy thing you can do is use sterile cotton for filtration. The majority of users I know are also smokers and they often use the filter tip of a cigarette for this purpose. There are two problems with this. First, even the unused filter tips are not clean. They are more than adequate for the process of smoking tobacco, but injecting heroin is a bit more invasive a procedure. Second, the filter tips are not necessarily pure cotton and could contain harmful chemicals or even particles.

Both of these simple things can greatly reduce your risk when injecting heroin. The most common reason that people give for not doing them is that they require too much preparation. But the fact is that heroin doesn't generally just fall into your lap. Acquiring it takes preparation. Getting clean syringes and cotton are very easy in comparison. There is no good reason not to follow these recommendations. Responsible use requires it.

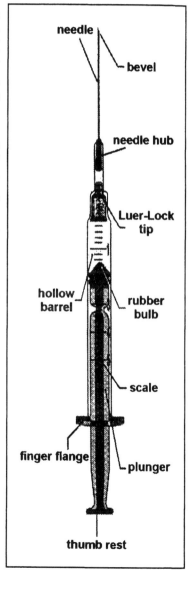

Figure 4
A syringe with each part labeled.

Exactly what constitutes a clean syringe is not as obvious as it may appear: a clean syringe is one that has not come into contact with *any* substance except that which you wish to inject into your body. Clearly, this is ideal. Once a sterile syringe is removed from its packaging, it is no longer sterile and it is under constant assault by contaminants. Our purpose is to keep the syringe as clean as possible, bearing in mind that perfect cleanliness (sterility) is an ideal that we strive for but cannot attain.

In order to inject a pure substance (heroin along with any other garbage that it's been cut with), you must start with a sterile syringe. This does not mean a syringe that only you've used. Once a syringe has been used, it is definitely no longer clean. It has been in contact with your skin, vein, and blood, which serve as a breeding ground for bacteria, which you do not want injected back into your body.

What is even more important than this self-contamination is the fact that the longer a syringe is in the open (outside its sterile container), the more likely it is to become contaminated. Remember that even in the cleanest houses, you are in a veritable sea of dust particles. A large fraction of that dust is the dead skin cells of all of the people who have been in the house during the previous years. Dust particles are another breeding ground for bacteria and they are excellent transport vehicles for viruses. Both viruses and bacteria can kill you. For now, just remember that improper needle technique can kill you and this should be sufficient motivation to use the best technique available.

Acquiring Syringes

For the majority of users, all of this talk of clean syringes may seem moot because syringes are illegal in most places. This is bad of course, but not a rationalization for using dirty syringes. There are two things that can be done in this case: get an illegal or semi-legal supply of clean syringes or clean your own. Many places have needle exchange programs that can help. Needle exchanges are not the best of all worlds, however. They are usually inconveniently located, open a small number of hours per week, and limit the number of exchanges on a single visit. In addition, you must still get some needles to exchange in the first place.

The street price of a syringe is $2.00 in San Francisco and New York. They are usually bought from different people than the heroin itself, but are still exchanged with the same secrecy and fear of law-enforcement. In my experience, needle vendors are usually not junkies — in San Francisco they are usually crack addicts. Even though the mark-up on syringes is large, it isn't unreasonable to buy them on the street if you are not using a lot of heroin.

There are a few things you should remember when you buy syringes on the street. The first is that every city has slang for syringes, so you may have some trouble communicating. In San Francisco, syringes are known as "outfits" and dealers will usually give you a blank look if you request "rigs." If you get a blank look, just rattle off a list of synonyms until the blank look dissipates. Check the glossary for synonyms of syringe.

Another issue that is applicable to buying anything on the street is that no price is set in stone. Dealers will always try to get full price, especially if they don't think much of you. The game is the same as at a garage sale: tell them that you only have however much money. It is often possible to get a syringe for $1.00. Just remember that the syringes you are buying are almost always acquired for free at needle exchanges. You can also get bulk discounts. Ten syringes should never cost you more than $10.00.

The last and most important issue regarding buying syringes on the street is making sure that you are buying clean syringes. Some people will sell you dirty syringes, especially very late at night. You decrease your chances of getting ripped off in this way by making sure that the dealer has the syringe bag (syringes are packaged in bags of ten and forty). Also, you can buy an entire sealed bag of ten. One way to tell if a syringe is clean is to see if you can push the plunger in. New syringes have their plungers pulled out by about a sixteenth of an inch. This is no guarantee either way, but it is a good indication.

A better and cheaper option than buying syringes on the street is to import your own. Some places do not regulate syringes. Do you ever go to any of these places? If so, it is a simple matter to pick up a couple hundred syringes, which should last you a year or more, depending upon how much you use. Another approach is to get a friend to mail you a box. This is illegal, but the lack of any smell makes such a process relatively safe. The main thing to remember here is that it is relatively easy to get a supply and once you have a supply you can replenish it with needle exchange programs or by repeating your importation process.

The Injection Process

The process of shooting up has four stages: preparing the syringe, finding a location, injecting, and cleaning up. The reason that most intravenous users do so much damage to their veins is that they do not spend enough time with the second step, which is the most critical. When I was a junkie, I destroyed my veins because I was impatient. At worst, I would jab myself a hundred times before finding a vein. If you want to cure yourself of a needle fixation, this is a good way to do it — it doesn't take much of this kind of self-mutilation to start believing that injection is just not pleasant. When a good vein is chosen, it greatly simplifies the injection process. The other steps are easy.

Preparing the Syringe

The process is pretty simple, in theory. It goes like this: the heroin is poured into a spoon or other receptacle. Water is added to it and the mixture is heated and stirred so that the heroin is completely dissolved in the water. This mixture is drawn into the syringe through a piece of cotton, which acts as a particulate filter. Air bubbles are removed and you're all done.

It is important that the spoon be clean. Obviously, you can't buy a sterile spoon in its own little sterile bag the way you can syringes. If you want to be as safe as possible, the spoon should be boiled, air dried, and used. You are doing well even if you simply wash and dry your spoon before each use. Under no circumstances share your spoon with another user for the same reasons that you should not share syringes. This doesn't matter if everyone always uses clean syringes, but it is easy to get mixed up: some user may reuse a syringe, and you may get infected. Make sure that you have your own spoon and don't allow others to use it.

Before starting, wash your hands. If you can manage it, take a shower. You can pass along bacteria and viruses from your own body, and taking a shower is an easy way to cut down on your risk. This is particularly true if you are ill.

Get a clean glass and fill it with clean water or, better still, use boiled water. Pour the heroin into your clean spoon. Draw a small amount of water (e.g., 0.5 cc) into the syringe and dispense it into the spoon. The exact amount of water will depend upon the amount of heroin you are trying to dissolve and your preference for solution concentration. Lay the syringe over the top of the glass, making sure not to allow the needle to touch it.

You will want to use a high temperature flame to heat the mixture because, by and large, the higher the temperature of the flame, the cleaner it is. And the cleaner the flame, the less likely that impurities from the combustion process will end up in the mixture. The problem with these impurities is that contaminants from the room can adhere to them thus causing the usual problems with hygiene.

There are many options as far as flames go. It is pretty hard to buy a decent disposable lighter these days. Almost all lighters are childproof which means they are a pain to use. In addition, I end up throwing out about half of them without ever using them (not because they're childproof, but because they aren't made well). There are alternatives, of course. There are Zippo lighters, which have many advantages; they provide a wind-resistant flame, they can stand up by themselves while "on," and they are attractive, if that's important to you. The disadvantages are that they are relatively expensive and you have to reload the lighter fluid. There is almost nothing good to be said of matches; they burn out quickly and provide a low temperature flame, although using several matches at once helps. On the plus side, they are cheap and easy to obtain. Probably the best flame is that of a gas stove, if you have one.

The spoon is heated so that the water in it just begins to boil. Limiting the heating process to the beginning of a boil is a compromise between greater hygiene (by allowing the boil to continue) and less heroin loss (heroin is quite soluble in water even without heating the solution). Depending upon your desires and needs, you may want to heat the solution more or less. Now use the rubber bulb from the syringe to stir the mixture until it is completely dissolved. Do not use the syringe needle because it dulls the bevel and makes injecting harder — increasing the likelihood of vein damage.

Once the heroin is completely dissolved, add a small piece (about an eighth-inch in diameter) of clean cotton to the solution. You can buy packages of cotton balls, part of which may be used as a filter while the rest may be used to clot the injection site. Make sure that the cotton balls are 100% cotton. There are mixed fiber cotton balls and while these will work, they do not hold together well, filter poorly, and are generally harder to use.

Set the spoon with the solution down on a solid surface. You may want to lay down a tissue on the table because the bottom of the spoon can be quite sooty. The poorer the flame, the dirtier the spoon will be and subsequent firings will increase the dirt. Draw the mixture out of the spoon through the cotton and into the syringe. The cotton ball acts as a filter for larger impurities. Try to avoid letting the needle tunnel through the cotton and make contact with the spoon since this will damage the syringe tip and eliminate the filtration process.

It is possible to accomplish this process while holding the spoon. Under most circumstances, this kind of "cocktail party" juggling is unnecessary. The procedure takes a little practice and skill but it is not beyond most people. It is mostly just a matter of holding the syringe with your first and second fingers and pulling the plunger back with the thumb of the same hand. Alternatively, you may hold the syringe with the second finger and thumb and pull the plunger back with your first finger. Another alternative is to have a partner. The process goes very smoothly between couples who are used to each other.

Keeping a syringe clean through the process of preparing it takes constant vigilance. You must be constantly on the lookout for ways in which you may be contaminating your syringe.

Now that the syringe is filled, you need to remove the air bubbles from it. Contrary to popular belief, injecting a small air bubble will not kill you. If enough air is injected (a half cc or more), then you can die, but this is pretty hard to do by accident. You should try to remove all of the air from the syringe before inject-

ing, just don't get too freaked out that there may be a tiny air bubble in your syringe that you do not see.

Hold the syringe with the tip pointed up. Tap the syringe repeatedly to get the air bubbles to the top and the solution to the bottom. This may also be accomplished by pressing the syringe
firmly with your thumb and letting it slide off — this is a motion
similar to snapping your fingers. Then press in the plunger slowly
until all of the air has been released from the syringe; you will
know that you have reached this point because the solution will
begin to come out of the syringe tip. If you do not wish to lose any
of the solution, leave a little air at the top.

If you are not going to inject right away, it is best to place the
plastic syringe tip cover back over the needle. There are various
methods of doing this but most of them will get you stuck. I recommend the one-hand method. Place the cap open-end up onto a
stable horizontal surface such as a table. Hold the syringe, needle
end pointing downward, about halfway up the barrel with your
thumb, first, and second fingers. Slowly lower the syringe onto the
cap. Doing this requires good eyesight and it may help to move
your head close to the cap. With experience, you will be able to
put the cap back on the syringe without even allowing the needle
to graze the inside edges of the cap.

Finding a Location

That completes the process of preparing the syringe. Now we
move on to finding a location for the injection. For an intravenous
injection, this is the most challenging aspect of administering heroin: choosing a suitable vein. For the other two methods, this is
relatively simple.

Intravenous: For a user who has never or very rarely mainlined,
finding a vein is relatively easy. For a junkie, doing so can be an
exercise in frustration. Patience is the key to success in all cases.

Most people are confused about the difference between veins
and arteries — ignorance of this distinction can cause you great
harm, or at least great pain. Arteries bring oxygenated blood from
the heart to various parts of the body while veins collect and return
the de-oxygenated or "used" blood back to the heart and lungs.
The color of blood depends upon whether it has oxygen in it or

not. Blood that has oxygen is red (this is why when you cut yourself the blood is always red — it gets oxygenated by the air once it leaves your body). Blood that does not have oxygen is blue or purple. Thus, arteries are red (when you can see them) and veins are blue; veins tend to be larger and more numerous than arteries, and because of their lack of a strong muscular wall, do not "pulse."

Since veins tend to be close to the surface and arteries do not, it is unlikely that you will purposefully inject into an artery. But be careful, there are some arteries close to the surface — always check for a pulse. The biggest problem is injecting too deeply into a vein, going through it and inadvertently injecting into an artery, since veins and arteries often lie close to one another. There is no ironclad way of knowing that you are hitting a vein instead of an artery — this is one of the risks that you must accept if you are to use this method of administration.

Once you know what a vein is, it is relatively easy to find one to use, at least for an infrequent user. By and large you will inject into your arm (see Figure 5). Some people inject into their leg but this is usually because they have run out of usable places on their arms to inject. Others inject there because it is easier to control and requires less dexterity because both hands can be used. It has a disadvantage that veins on the leg are not usually as prominent as they are on the arms. Still others inject into the neck but this is a very dangerous injection site.

There is a widely held belief that injecting into the neck gives the greatest rush of all injection sites. This is based on the fallacious belief that the heroin is transported directly to the brain from the neck. This, however, would only be the case if you were injecting into an artery, which you should *never* do.[1] Instead, the heroin must be injected into a *vein* in the neck, where it is transported back to the heart and then to the brain. Given that the distance from the neck to the heart is smaller than the distance from the arm to the heart, the rush from a neck injection should be very

---

[1] Injecting into an artery in the neck can cause facial paralysis and conceivably, death.

slightly more intense. Similarly, a leg injection should be very slightly less intense. However, I have never noticed much of a difference. Issues such as drug purity and quantity are certainly more important than injection location.

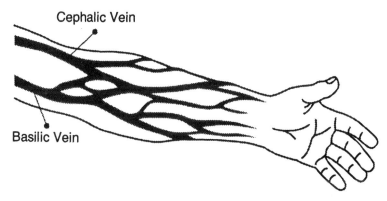

Figure 5
The main veins of the arm.

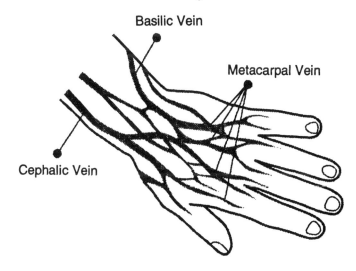

Figure 6
The main veins of the hand.

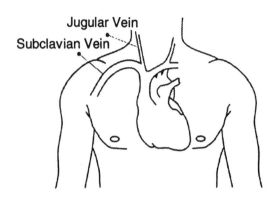

Figure 7
The veins of the chest and neck.

In order to make the veins stand out so that you can make the best vein choice, you should use a tie-off. This involves restricting the flow of blood to and from your arm in order to cause the veins to protrude. To do this, take a long piece of rope or rubber or cloth and wrap it around the limb roughly half way between your elbow and your shoulder. This, in itself, does not make the veins stand out particularly well, so once you are tied off you should make a tight fist and release it about five or ten times. This will cause the veins to become quite prominent.

There are a couple of other things that you can do to make the veins stand out. The first is to massage the area in which you wish to inject. This should be done in the direction of venous flow — that is, away from the extremity of your body. Another technique is to lightly tap the vein with your finger. Do not do this with too much force — veins are delicate and you can injure them in this manner. A final suggestion is to use heat. Veins, like most materials, shrink when cold. Your veins will stand out more if you apply heat to them. This can be done by simply taking a hot shower. But areas may be selectively heated with the use of a moist towel or a blow dryer.

Later, I'll discuss some options for users with bad veins, but first I want to go over the procedure for the user with good veins. You are best off sticking with the largest vein that you can find.

This is primarily because it is easiest to inject into a large vein with confidence that you will actually hit the vein and not inject into muscular tissue. If you have ever given blood and you remember what vein they used to draw the blood from, then use that vein. This vein is the basilic. The other main vein of the arm is the cephalic. Both of these veins are located at the back of your elbow. Most of the veins on the forearms and hands are branches of these two veins.

These large veins at the back of the elbow are the easiest places to inject. And if you inject infrequently — less than once a week — they are likely the only veins that you will need to inject into. Note however, that should you scar these areas, it will be noticed when giving blood and also probably when having blood pressure checks. The positive side is that minor abrasions in these areas most likely will be considered the result of bad technique from a previous medical procedure.

If these veins are not available, you still have many choices. The hands, for example, can be very rewarding. The downside is that the hands are a very public part of the body. Scars on the hands are very noticeable, especially on fair-skinned people. Each digit of the hand gets its blood supply from the metacarpal veins. The metacarpal veins are branches of the basilic vein (2nd, 3rd, and 4th fingers) and the cephalic vein (thumb, 1st, and 2nd fingers). Each finger has a fairly substantial vein associated with it — this makes finding the veins relatively easy. The best of these veins is the metacarpal, which runs up the side of the first finger, just past the thumb. The easiest place to inject into any of these veins is before they reach the fingers. Once they have reached the fingers they are much smaller and harder to hit (See Figure 6).

If you are having a hard time finding good veins in which to inject, spend a little time in a hot shower. Massage your arms and experiment with cutting off the flow to various areas. The time you spend doing this will greatly expand your knowledge of the venous system in your arm. You will probably also be surprised at the good veins that show up.

You may want to experiment with the veins in your legs and feet. They are good locations if you are concerned about anyone finding out that you inject drugs. Most of what I have said about finding veins in the arm applies to the legs as well.

The main veins in the leg are the great saphenous and femoral veins. In most people, the great saphenous vein can be located down the entire leg from thigh to ankle. It offers the easiest injection site in the leg and, even with a moderate injection frequency, can last a user a lifetime. The great saphenous vein is most easy to find in the ankle (especially in thin people), but be very careful injecting into the ankle since there are many surface arteries here.

One of the largest veins in the body is the subclavian vein, which carries de-oxygenated blood from the arms directly into the heart. This vein runs roughly parallel to your shoulders (See Figure 7). It is dangerous to attempt to inject into this vein. It is relatively deep, thus increasing the difficulty in finding it; it also increases the chance of injecting into an artery; and you may also puncture your lung and cause a pneumothorax (a partially collapsed lung) which is quite painful and potentially life threatening.

A vein of last resort is the jugular vein in the neck. The neck is a place to avoid injecting because there are many surface arteries, which you may inadvertently hit, an obviously, the location of this vein prevents the use of a tourniquet. Instead, before the injections, the user closes his mouth and blows out but without letting any airflow — a similar procedure used by many people to neutralize the air pressure behind the eardrum. This may cause one's cheeks to expand like Dizzy Gillespie playing the trumpet. In addition to this, the veins in the neck will stand out. Make sure that you check that you are injecting into a vein — *make sure it has no pulse*. The whole procedure is difficult to accomplish, especially alone. One of the biggest problems is holding your breath for as long as the injection procedure takes.

I have mentioned vein rolling a couple of times already and finding a vein that is not likely to roll is very important. One good aspect of deeper veins is that they stay put. If you inject into the right spot your syringe needle will enter the vein. But extremely superficial veins do not have enough of a muscular foundation to remain immobile. So, when a needle enters the skin on top of them, the vein moves to the side and the needle enters the flesh below the vein. It is easy to tell how mobile a vein is: simple push down on it lightly. If the vein moves to the side, consider another vein.

Intramuscular and Subcutaneous: If you are doing intramuscular injections, then the process is almost the opposite of that for intravenous injections. You should look for a location that does not have a large or many veins. Find a nice fleshy muscle. The two places you normally get vaccinations are good: the shoulder and buttock.

For a subcutaneous injection, you have even more liberty than with an intramuscular injection. Basically, any location will work but you will prefer a location where the skin is fairly loose so that the injection is not painful.

Injection

Before injecting, it is very important to clean your hands and the area around the injection site with isopropyl alcohol. I am assuming that you have already washed your hands and arms with soap and water. Saturate a clean cotton ball (or you can use a packaged alcohol swab) with rubbing alcohol and clean the area around where you plan to inject. Then, clean the fingers of the hand that will do the injecting. Then wait for a minute or so, since injecting into alcohol saturated skin is painful.

Intravenous: There are a couple of techniques for doing the actual injecting, depending upon circumstances. If you have a good solid vein that will not roll, you may inject right into the top of the vein. If you have a vein that is not so well-behaved, you are better off injecting into it sideways. I have argued about this procedure with phlebotomists who consider it completely unacceptable. But this is because they are trained to look for a vein that they can inject properly. If you have bad veins you have no such luxury.

Rolling veins can be dealt with if you can get a partner to help you. Have your partner press down on the vein you are injecting into a few inches on either side of the site of injection. In addition to pressing down on the vein, the partner should pull the vein on either side away from the injection site. This will hold the vein steady and keep it from rolling.

If you have a solid vein, place the syringe tip against the skin above the vein directed toward the interior of the body (in the direction of blood flow). Push the syringe in at about a 30 degree angle (this is one-third of perpendicular). This will sting a little, but should not hurt a great deal. When you think that you are in the center of the vein, stop. If you are injecting into the side of the vein, you still want to be oriented about 30 degrees relative to the vein. How many degrees sideways your injection is will depend upon the vein. You want the needle to be pushing the vein in a direction that the vein will not move. Again, once you think you are inside the vein, stop.

With the syringe tip inside the vein, pull the plunger out slightly. If you are in the vein, this will cause blood to flow into the syringe. This is called the "pull back" and it is a good test to make sure that you are injecting into your vein and not into your flesh. It is not foolproof, however: if you are in an artery, for example, it will look the same. Similarly, if you are in the subcutaneous layer it will look the same. So you must take care to keep good control of where your needle is.

If blood flows into the syringe and you feel reasonably confident that you are in a vein, push the plunger in a little way and wait ten seconds. If you are in an artery, this will give your body plenty of time to react to the injection. You will know that you have injected into an artery because it will hurt. This pain is *not* felt at the injection site — if you feel a burning at the injection site it is because you are injecting into a muscle. The sensation of injecting into an artery is usually very similar to an electric shock at your fingertips. If you appear to be in an artery, pull the syringe out and raise your arm over your head if the pain continues. Similarly, if a bubble forms under your skin, you are in the subcutaneous layer.

If you don't feel any discomfort from the initial injection and no bubble forms, slowly push in the plunger until its contents are emptied. A half cc of solution should take between five and ten seconds, but don't worry too much if it takes longer. The main issue is that if you inject too rapidly you can cause the vein to rupture. Remove the syringe, put a clean cotton ball onto the entry site and press. Remove the tie from your upper arm. Put the syringe someplace safe and get into a comfortable position.

Some users remove the tourniquet before injecting and certainly this is the "proper" procedure — it is better to do this if you can manage it. The problem is that it is harder. Often, taking the tourniquet off causes the needle tip to slip out of the vein. Instead, you may inject the needle into a likely spot, remove the tourniquet and then do the pull back when you think you are inside the vein. To start, however, you should leave the tourniquet on but make sure that your injection site is at least a foot from it. As you become more proficient with the injection process, you can try injecting without the tourniquet.

Intramuscular and Subcutaneous: Push the needle into the muscle about a quarter of an inch. Do a syringe pull back just like an intravenous injection. In this case you do *not* want the syringe to fill with blood. If blood does not flow into the syringe, it indicates that you are neither in a vein nor an artery. When you flush the contents of the syringe, do so slowly. How slowly will depend upon your body. Injecting quickly hurts but it also does not give the muscle time to react to the infusion of heroin. As a result, you will put a pool of solution into your muscle, which will actually cause your body to absorb the heroin more slowly than if you had injected more slowly. Taking thirty seconds to empty the syringe is not unreasonable.

When you pull the syringe plunger back and get nothing, you are not pulling air into the syringe. That empty space in the syringe is just that; empty, it is a vacuum. So don't be afraid of injecting it into your body — you won't be injecting anything at all. That vacuum in the syringe does create a negative pressure, however, and this pressure stresses the tissue you are injecting into. As a result of this, it is best to limit the extent of your pull back as much as possible. The farther you pull back, the greater the negative pressure and therefore the greater the potential for tissue damage.

Injecting subcutaneously starts very similarly to intramuscular injection. Inject into the muscle tissue and perform a pull back. You should get no blood in the syringe. Now pull the syringe out of the tissue slowly. When you reach the layer of blood vessels under the skin, the syringe will fill with blood. At this point you should stop — this illustrates the need to remove the syringe very slowly since this layer is very thin and you may fill the syringe with blood, only to pull it out of your body altogether. Then you must start the procedure over.

Any time you perform a pull back, get blood in the syringe, and then lose your blood vessel layer (or vein) you complicate matters greatly. Once blood is inside the syringe, you have a time constraint because the solution will clot and become useless. When this happens, it is important to remain calm. Getting excited will only make matters worse. If you took my previous suggestion of limiting the size of your pull back, you will have given yourself extra time because the smaller the amount of blood the slower the clotting process. Generally it takes several minutes, even under the worst conditions. So just start over and take your time.

Cleanup

If you do things as I recommend, there is relatively little cleanup to do: simply dispose of the syringe. Unfortunately, disposing of a syringe takes some care because syringes are dangerous objects — you can't just throw them into a trash can. In most places, you cannot dispose of a syringe as "hazardous material" because syringes are illegal and you don't want to be arrested for protecting society. Society has chosen to make syringes illegal and so it must accept the consequences when syringes are not disposed of in the best way possible.

Syringe Disposal: On the other hand, there is no reason to put others in danger because of your recreational choices. Disposing of a syringe is a three-step process: destroy, contain, and dispose. Destroying consists of making the syringe unusable and less dangerous to anyone who might handle it. Containing consists of putting the syringe in some kind of receptacle, which hinders a person from unwittingly handling the syringe. Disposing, in this case, consists of throwing the contained syringes away so that they cannot be traced back to the user.

You greatly limit the danger of a dirty syringe by removing the needle and storing it in a safe place. Most syringe exchange programs recommend that you do this by breaking the needle off inside the syringe cap. To do this, place the cap back on the syringe (see Preparing the Syringe, earlier in this chapter). Hold the syringe by its barrel with the capped needle pointing downward at a 45° angle. Jam the syringe downward onto a tabletop. This action will cause the needle and its plastic base to break off inside the cap.

Another approach is to break off the syringe tip by hand, but be careful not to poke yourself. This should only be done on your own syringes — don't take chances with those of others. Remove the syringe plunger, drop the needle inside the barrel, and put the plunger back in. This will cause the needle to be trapped between the plunger and the inside syringe barrel wall. Over time, the needle may work itself out, but it is in a fairly stable position, which keeps the needle from harming someone.

After the syringe has been destroyed, it should be stored in some kind of container, which will hold a large number of syringes. This serves two purposes: it keeps all of the used syringes in a single location and it acts as another barrier between the used syringes and a person who might get hurt by one. A good choice is an empty coffee can with a plastic top. Almost anything that is convenient will work, but stay away from things like paper bags, which tear easily.

Before you dispose of your syringe container, wipe it clean of fingerprints. You may think that this is overly cautious, but I spent six months in jail for possession of 63 syringes. Don't underestimate the level of hysteria that a large number of syringes can generate. It is also a good idea to wipe the syringes themselves clean before you put them in the container.

Be careful where you dispose of your syringe container. Remember that law enforcement is now allowed to go through your garbage, so you are best off if you dispose of any incriminating property discreetly in a public place (shopping mall bathrooms are good). Don't use the same place repeatedly, because it puts you in a dangerous position and never have any illegal substances with you when you dispose of the syringes.

Cleaning Syringes: I don't recommend cleaning syringes for a number of reasons. First, it is very difficult to get a syringe clean. The process of cleaning syringes destroys the metal of the syringe. Second, as syringes are used they become dull. Dull syringes make injecting yourself difficult, they cause great damage to your veins, and they leave nasty scars. Although you may see "old fashioned" syringes with replaceable points in movies, the fact is that *everyone* uses disposable syringes.

Sometimes you have no choice but to reuse syringes, however. The sooner after use that you clean your syringe, the better off you are. This is not as bad as it sounds. A few rinses with water will remove the vast majority of the matter in the syringe. This can usually be done even when mainlining — before the rush begins. In order to do this, draw clean water into the syringe — at least as much water as you had solution. Flush the contents of the syringe into a waste container. Repeat the process at least two more times.

There is an important thing to remember about this process. When you draw water into a used syringe, the water in the container from which you drew it is no longer clean. As a result, if you are using with other people, each person should have his own water container. Otherwise, it is very easy to use contaminated water.

When you have time, you can do the detailed syringe cleaning. Start by rinsing the tip and the barrel. Disassemble the syringe and rinse it thoroughly with clean water. Then reassemble it and draw clean water into the syringe and flush it. Repeat this several times. This will make sure that the needle is mostly clean. Repeat this entire rinsing process with a pure bleach solution (you should use rubber gloves when doing this).[2]

Heat about two quarts of water in a clean pan. When the water has reached a boil turn the heat down so that the water is just barely boiling (the temperature of the water will be the same regardless of whether the water is boiling slowly or fast). This will assure that you will not boil off all of the water. Place the syringes

---

[2] There is some indication that bleach does not destroy the hepatitis virus, but that hydrogen peroxide does. You could rinse with both.

in the water and let them boil for 15 minutes. Remove them with tongs, making sure that you hold the syringe capsule by its body and the plunger by its handle. Insert the plunger into the syringe capsule. Put the cover over the syringe tip.

Snorting

Snorting is a popular ingestion technique when the available heroin is distributed as a powder. In general, this is the case on the east coast of the U.S. On the west coast, where black tar is the common form of heroin, snorting is not as popular and some users are even unaware that it is possible to snort heroin. A similar east/west dichotomy exists for smoking, as white powder users rarely smoke heroin.

Inhalation is probably the least intimidating of the three main ingestion methods. To a new user, snorting does not even seem like taking a drug, probably because it is so bizarre. In addition there is a natural progression of illegal drug usage from marijuana to cocaine to heroin (this is actually not so "normal," as discussed in Chapter One). For most people, it does not take too much courage to switch from snorting one white powder to another.

When cocaine was widely used, it was popular to use rolled up dollar bills in place of a straw. I have never abided the "you don't know where that dollar bill's been" school of thought — as if people were using money for toilet paper or something. But I don't go too far in the other direction. Money does touch a lot of different hands and most hands are not what I would want stuck up my nose. So use a clean straw about two inches long and don't share it.

The heroin is poured onto a ridged solid surface. Perhaps the best is glass. Years ago, I spent a dollar buying a one square foot pane of glass. I covered the edges with a couple of layers of duct tape so that I didn't cut myself or anyone else. This works wonderfully for snorting; indeed it makes an excellent working surface for any heroin-related ingestion task.

Since powdered heroin is generally lumpy it must be diced with a razor blade. You have undoubtedly seen this done by cocaine users in movies. After the dicing, the heroin is divided into lines. The purpose of this is to divide the large quantity of drug into portions so that a group may equitably share it. Otherwise, the lines are useless. There is no trouble snorting from a mound. In fact, a mound is preferable because it is not necessary to move the straw around. Additionally, it is particularly easy to pour an amount into the corner of a small box — it can be snorted directly from there.

To snort, put one end of the straw into your nose while you are away from the snorting surface. Exhale your breath. This is done so that you don't inadvertently blow the heroin off the surface. Holding your breath, bend your head down to the surface so that the other end of the straw touches the surface, but is about a quarter inch from the heroin. Now breath in through your nose. Take it easy — you don't want to do too much at once (it may be a good idea to select a small quantity from the entire amount and snort it). It is not necessary to close off your other nostril as this does little to help in the snorting process and gives you one more thing to worry about. For maximum effectiveness, you should alternate nostrils between subsequent snorts.

Snorting tar is harder, but the technique should be noted by powder users as well, because it provides a very nice way to use without worrying about maintaining a surface. Tar heroin, under most circumstances, cannot be diced the way that powder heroin can because tar heroin is gooey. Sometimes this is not the case — tar heroin can come in a more crystalline form (this is usually the case with heroin that has been cut with sugar), which can be diced. I've never seen anyone do this, however.

The process of snorting tar requires that the heroin be dissolved in water. If this sounds familiar, it should. It is the same procedure used to prepare heroin for injection. Syringes with the needle broken off are most commonly used. Eyedroppers work reasonably well although they have a tendency to leak. Nasal spray bottles are perhaps the best.

The actual snorting of this solution is a real pain, at least compared to snorting the powder. The tip of the container is placed inside the nose about a quarter of an inch. Now comes the tricky part. You must release the solution from the container at the same time that you suck in through your nose. If you screw up and the solution gets all over your face, just wipe it up with your fingers and shove it manually up your nose.

A couple of warnings about snorting: it's painful, it tastes bad, and it is still illegal. Cocaine is a local anesthetic, so snorting it does not hurt. You have no such advantage with heroin. Whether you snort powder or solution, be prepared. Also be prepared for what is usually a pretty bitter taste. The fact that you can easily snort heroin in public may make you bold, but never forget that this drug still has a very bad reputation and is still very illegal.

Smoking

Smoking is my favorite method of ingesting heroin. It is highly ritualistic and has more of a communal feel to it. But this is not always the case. I met one young couple who used to smoke heroin separately in a most wasteful manner. I don't know what bothered me more: the fact that they didn't use the drug to form any kind of human bond or the fact that they wasted so much of the heroin. I tried to explain to them that I could show them a better way, but they were happy with their own technique.

Smoking heroin can be done efficiently alone, but it is much easier as a couple. The basic idea is that heroin is placed on a surface which has a low heat capacity. A flame is applied to the surface from below in order to heat the heroin and start it boiling. This vapor is then inhaled with the help of some kind of tube. I will start by describing the smoking process for couples and then end with a few ideas on smoking alone.

Surface

The choice of a smoking surface is an important one. I have tried any number of surfaces and almost all have failed because they lacked a low heat capacity. What this means is that most surfaces heat up and cool down very slowly. An example of this is asphalt — even long after the sun has gone down, the asphalt, which has been heated by the sun all day, stays warm. So if you take even a relatively thin piece of glass (one-eighth inch thick) and apply a flame to it, it takes a long time for the glass to get really hot and once it is hot it takes a long time to cool down.

The perfect surface is one that gets hot the instant you apply a flame and cools off the instant you remove the flame. The reason you want this is that it allows you control of when the heroin is vaporized. When you apply the flame you want the smoker to be able to inhale the heroin vapor and when he is finished you want the heroin to quit boiling right away so that none is lost. This perfect surface exists in aluminum foil. It heats up quickly and cools down quickly and is generally a joy to use.

Tube

After the smoking surface, the most important decision you will need to make is what to use for a tube. I recommend toilet paper tubes. They are commonly available and they are large enough so that you are likely to lose very little smoke. It is possible, of course, that you will find something better. In fact, I've been looking for a large plastic tube for some time myself. But in all such endeavors you should use the toilet paper tube as the prototype. You do not want the tube to be too long because long tubes cause more smoke to stick to the tube and this increases loss. I have found that the width of the toilet paper tube is also perfect. Tubes that are too big or too small will result in loss. If the tube is too small, smoke will escape around the edges. If the tube is too large, it does not allow you to get good suction.

Couple's Procedure

There are several variations to smoking. In each, one person acts as the smoker and the other the helper. The main procedure is given below. The helper holds the foil flat and level. The foil should be about five inches by five inches so that it stays rigid when held from one side. The smoker pours a small amount of heroin onto the center of the foil. The helper then lets go of one end of the foil. With his free hand, he lights the lighter. The smoker puts the tube up to his mouth in a comfortable position and bends to a point where the end of the tube is roughly an inch directly over the heroin. The lighter is positioned directly below the heroin, underneath the foil (See Figure 8). When the smoker is nearly finished, he signals the helper, which tells him to remove the flame. The heroin will continue to smoke for as long as 2 seconds after the flame is removed. It takes a little while to get used to the exact timing, but before long you will be able to smoke with almost no direct loss using this procedure.

There are a few variations to this method of ingestion. The smoker can hold the foil. This has the advantage that it allows him immediate control of the flame; when he is finished he can simply pull away. The disadvantage is that it gives the smoker one more task. Another variation is to let the helper hold only the foil, letting the smoker hold the tube and the flame. If you have problems with the foil folding on you, then you might try this latter procedure. In my experience, it is very hard for the smoker to gauge where the flame is relative to the heroin, but some will no doubt be able to make this work.

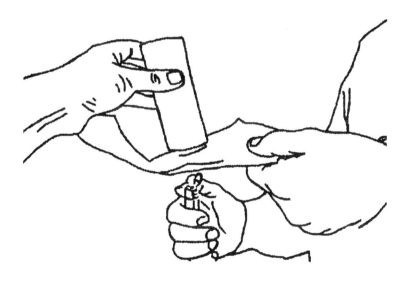

Figure 8
Proper heroin smoking procedure. The helper is holding the aluminum foil and the lighter while the smoker is holding the suction tube.

Solo Procedure

Most people who smoke heroin alone use a very small tube so that they can hold it in their mouths (generally a plastic straw), freeing their hands for holding the foil and the lighter. But due to the smallness of the tube, it is easy to lose much or even most of the heroin smoked. You may now be imagining holding a toilet paper roll in your mouth, but this is not how it's done — when your mouth is so contorted it is hard to inhale properly.

In order to smoke alone, you have to relinquish the hand's control of the flame, the foil, or the tube. As pointed out above, the tube is out. Luckily, there are reasonable methods using the other two. It is possible to use a couple of blocks, spaced about five inches apart, to hold the foil (some creative wire sculpting is also possible). Then you can use a lighter with one hand for the flame and hold the tube in the other.

I find the other method better. It involves the use of a stationary flame. The easiest example of this is a candle, although a Zippo lighter will also work. In this case you can hold the foil with one hand, the tube with the other and lower the foil toward the flame as you inhale. The downside of this method is that candle flames are very dirty and if you use one you will end up with a lot of soot. If you use a Zippo, you don't have to worry so much about soot, but you have to be very careful that the lighter does not fall over, and that if it does, it does not start a bigger fire.

Purifying Heroin

The impurities found in street heroin range from coffee to quinine to glass particles. Most impurities — like coffee — are harmless. You might even like some of them. Coffee, for example, can be tasted after injecting heroin that has been cut with it. Some impurities, like glass and even quinine, can be deadly. I strongly encourage you to remove the impurities from the heroin you buy. What follows is a three-step recipe that works despite the fact that it has been widely distributed on the Internet.

Removing Particulate Matter

The use of cotton for filtration while cooking heroin is a small attempt at purifying the heroin ingested. A much better job can be done, with a little hydrochloric acid (HCl). Place about a gram of heroin in a small glass container (a test tube is best, but any glassware that will allow mixing will work). Add a couple of drops of 28% hydrochloric acid and allow it to react for a couple of minutes. Next, add 5 ml of distilled water and mix vigorously so that everything dissolves.

At this point in the process, the heroin is in solution. The nonsoluble material in the container is garbage that you do not wish to ingest. Let the solution sit so that the particulate matter settles to the bottom and then withdraw the solution with a pipette, leaving the particulate matter behind. The simplest kind of pipette is an eyedropper. If a pipette is not available, it is possible to pour the solution out of one container into another, being careful not to allow any of the particulate matter to be transferred.

Removing Soluble Impurities

Add ammonium hydroxide to the solution, one drop at a time. This will cause a white precipitate to form. Continue adding the ammonium until you are certain that there is no more precipitate being formed. The solution is then gently mixed to assure that the ammonium is evenly distributed. At this point, the solution will have a milky look.

Now add the solution to about 100 ml of ethyl ether — a chemical with which great care must be taken, since it is quite combustible. Vigorously mix this new solution, and leave it to sit. The water will settle at the bottom of the container, where it can be removed with a pipette and then discarded.

Create a mixture of 5 ml of HCl and 5 ml distilled water and add it to the ethyl ether mixture. Stir it vigorously for several minutes. Afterwards, a water layer will form at the bottom of the container. You can then pipette this out and into a small container such as a petri dish.

Deacidification

Slowly add baking soda to the solution in the petri dish. This will cause the solution to bubble. When the bubbling stops, this process is finished. The resulting solution is then air-dried, which yields pure heroin and table salt (NaCl). The salt is harmless and may be ingested along with the heroin.

Final Thoughts

I have known plenty of chippers who inject. It is a mistake to think that how you get a drug into your body determines whether you are a responsible user (although most people think so). Any of the techniques that I've discussed in this chapter can be used in a safe and responsible manner. But I do have a few thoughts with which I would like to leave you.

Injecting is a method that I think you should stay away from. I don't say this because of any concerns about injection leading to addiction (it usually works the other way around). Nor do I say it because of any overdose concern (see Chapter Four). Hygiene is a major problem when injecting any substance, and I just don't think that the pros outweigh the cons. People do drugs to have a good time, and injecting takes away from this by adding a lot of concerns. If you aren't currently injecting, I recommend not starting. The only really compelling reason for injecting is that it will reduce your cost, but this is only a concern for someone who is doing too much heroin.

There is, of course, the mystery factor: the excitement of the unknown, the wish to be a "real" heroin user; and the thrill of experiencing the ultimate drug taboo. The first reason is easy to dispel. Despite what you may have heard, the high from injection is not substantially different than that from smoking, so there is no real mystery that needs to be discovered. If you only snort heroin, give smoking a try — it will give you a sense of the "heroin rush" and also get you higher than you are probably used to. If you're already smoking, you might work on improving your technique and try increasing your speed (if you work with a partner try not alternating for a change). Remember that regardless of how you administer heroin, it is still heroin.

I get very tired of the heroin mystique. You should not be using any drug to prove something. The reason that people think that heroin ought to be injected is because they think all junkies inject heroin (most do, but not all). Every drug can be injected and yet very few are associated with injection. Heroin is associated with injection because it is very expensive — which, in turn, is largely due to its reputation (this circles back on itself endlessly). Those who inject have no special claim to nobility in the heroin subculture — they only have a certain kinship with addicts, which is more a matter of concern — not joy.

Whenever your tolerance goes up, get concerned and set about reducing it. Never let your frequency increase, maintain a high level of hygiene quality, and rarely (if ever) inject heroin. You will be proud that you can say these things — they will speak well of you. And no one will ever question that you're a "real" user. *Anyone* who uses heroin is a "real" user.

There is not a lot to say about the thrill of experiencing the ultimate drug taboo. If you're set on it, go ahead and inject. But don't get it into your head that you have to inject all the time just because you've done it once or a few times. Injecting has its appeal and its occasional use is not a particularly bad idea. The risks are large, though, and as your normal administration technique, I would stay away from it.

In the end, it does not matter what technique you use as long as you are serious about using safely. Make sure that you read Chapter Four to find out about the problems associated with heroin use. As a heroin user, you are involved in a risky business. The moment you forget that, you greatly increase your risk.

Chapter Four
Risks

There are many risks you take as a heroin user: you may become physically addicted to it, you may get diseases from administering it, and you may overdose on it. But there is a lot that you can do to reduce the risks you take. In this chapter, I outline the main problems and suggest ways to avoid them.

Physical Addiction

When most people think of heroin, their bad opinion of the drug stems largely from fact that it is addictive. This stems from the fact that addiction in and of itself is thought to be bad. There is no rational reason for this belief. The belief originates, instead, from our puritanical heritage which holds that pleasure is bad. People become addicted to substances that give them pleasure, therefore addiction is bad.

There is one aspect of all addictions, which *is* bad: you have to worry about acquiring it. Coffee drinkers have to make sure that they have coffee in the house before they go to bed so that they can get their fix in the morning just like heroin addicts. If you go on a trip you have to make sure that you bring your drug with you or that you can acquire it wherever you are going. I don't like this and this is the main reason that I'm not addicted to any drugs, even the supposed soft drugs.

The truth is that we are a nation of caffeine addicts. This addiction does little harm because the drug is legal and inexpensive.[1] But heroin is both illegal and expensive, so there are negative effects of heroin addiction. The more heroin you use, the more you expose yourself to law enforcement and the more likely it is that you will find yourself in jail. The high price of heroin causes two primary problems. First, it forces users to inject (or even just smoke or snort) the drug instead of taking it orally, which increases your risk of disease and overdose. Second, it usually means that you will have to devote most of your time to acquiring money to support your habit.

There is one aspect of heroin addiction that society does not consider a problem but which, from the user's standpoint eclipses all but one other: as an addict, you really don't get high. Addicts tend to build their habits up to a level that meets their financial resources. Once there, it is rare to have enough money to get more than your usual dose, and so you rarely get high — instead, you get "well."

The biggest problem with addiction is withdrawal. If you do not get enough of your daily supply, you will get sick. There are many reasons why you may be forced into withdrawal: you may not have enough money; the drugs may not be available; the drugs may be available but at such a low level of purity that they don't help you much; or you may be incarcerated. The symptoms of heroin withdrawal are many and varied. The most important, or painful, are: depression, insomnia, nausea, vomiting, diarrhea, and abdominal cramps. In addition, you will likely experience many of the following: anxiety, irritability, lacrimation (watery eyes), general body aches, restlessness, perspiration, dilated pupils, "goose

---

[1] There was an attempt by Congress to outlaw caffeine in the 1930s but it was by then a practical impossibility due to fact that so many products had caffeine in them. The idea that caffeine is a safe drug is also groundless. An IV dose of 3 g of caffeine is lethal. Compare this to cocaine, which requires 1.2 g — less, but not that much less. It takes about 8 g of caffeine, ingested orally, to die.

flesh," hot flashes, gagging, fever, increased heart rate, increased blood pressure, dehydration, weight loss, nervousness, hyperactivity, leg cramps, and alternating profuse sweating and chills.

The truth is that you can do a lot of heroin without becoming physically addicted to it. In order to become physically addicted, you must get your body used to the drug being around. If you allow the drug to leave your body before you use again, your body will not become physically dependent upon it.

There are many theories to explain why the body becomes physically addicted to some substances. Most of these theories are quite technical in addition to being flawed in many ways. The most compelling theory is called Homeostasis. The idea of this theory is that the body tries to regulate itself, always maintaining equilibrium. When a drug is ingested, the body adapts to its presence in an attempt to get back to its idea of the body's biological equilibrium.

A good example will go a long way toward explaining this concept. Morphine causes the body to become constipated. The body, in response, attempts to become unconstipated by releasing certain anti-constipating chemicals — just as it would if this were due to some kind of an illness. If the heroin is done continuously for long enough, the body gets used to it and automatically creates these anti-constipation chemicals. When the heroin is taken away, the body continues to create those chemicals even though it is no longer fighting against a constipating drug. The result: diarrhea (a common withdrawal effect). This condition will continue until the body adjusts to its new (no heroin) state.

This is a great over-simplification of the process, of course. But this theory is helpful in that it is, at least, generally correct and as a model of the functioning of the body, it works quite well. The main problem that scientists have with the Homeostatic Theory is that it does not provide a mechanism for the body's adaptation to the drug. This is an important issue but it does not affect us in our discussion.

What this theory of addiction tells us is that if we let the heroin get out of our body, we will not become physically addicted. So how often can heroin be taken? There are actually two questions here. First, we need to know how often we can do heroin over long periods of time. In other words, can we do it every day? Every other day? Every week? Second, we need to know how long we can use heroin continuously before becoming addicted. In other words, how long does it take for the body to adapt to the presence of heroin?

In order to discuss the first issue, we need a little data. Table 1 is adapted from an article by Foley and Inturrisi.[2] It presents the pain-relieving properties of various opioids relative to each other. In the first column is the drug name, the next columns contain its potency relative to morphine when injected intramuscularly, potency relative to morphine when taken orally, and the halflife of the drug. In each case, the table indicates how many milligrams (mg) of the drug would have to be taken to achieve the same effect as 100 mg of morphine administered intramuscularly.

Table 1: A comparison of the analgesic strength of selected opiates and opioids when administered intramuscularly (IM) and orally (Oral). The last column contains the halflife of each drug in hours.*Note that the halflife of heroin is only three *minutes* after which time it has broken down into morphine, primarily.

Drug	IM	Oral	Halflife
Codeine	1300	2000	2-3
Hydrocodone	200	400	3-4
Oxycodone	150	300	2-3
Morphine	100	600	2-3
Heroin	50	400	2-3*
Hydromorphone	15	75	2-3
Methadone	100	200	15-190
Oxymorphone	10	100	2-3
Levorphanol	20	40	12-15

The column that most concerns us here is the halflife. The halflife is the amount of time that it takes your body to remove

[2] *The Little Book of Opium*, by Francis Moraes and Debra Kita, Ronin Publishing, Berkeley, 2001.

half of the drug that is in your system. The reason we use this odd kind of standard is that it is not possible to say how long a drug will stay in the body. The amount of a drug that your body removes in a given period of time is dependent upon how much is already there. Think of the drug in your body as dirt on your carpet. If you run the vacuum over it once, you get a lot of the dirt. Run it over the carpet again and you will get more dirt out, but not as much as you did on the first pass. Similarly, the third pass will not yield as much dirt as the second pass. This is how your body works: the more of a drug that is in your body, the more it will remove. The amount of time it takes your system to remove half of the drug in your body is called the halflife.

Note a curious feature of this: your body does not "remember" how much drug it used to have inside it. Let's look at a concrete example. Suppose that you have a blood alcohol level of 0.08. Your body does not care if its alcohol level got that way because you just drank it up to that level or because you had been much more drunk and you stopped drinking so that some of the alcohol has been removed. In either case, if you do not drink any more, your blood alcohol level will be 0.04 (half of 0.08) after one alcohol halflife.

Let's say that you ingest 400 mg of morphine. Since the halflife of morphine is three hours, the amount of morphine in your body will go down in an exponential manner. This means that after three hours there will be 200 mg of morphine floating around in your body. After six hours, 100 mg; nine hours, 50 mg; twelve hours, 25 mg., and so on. The main point here is that regardless of how much morphine you ingest, half of it will be removed from your body within about three hours.

A study done on rats indicated that they could be given Levorphanol every 48 hours without the onset of physical addiction or even increased tolerance. Levorphanol has a halflife of twelve hours *for humans*. Rats have a substantially faster metabolism rate. In order to be relatively safe (and to make the math easier) let's assume that the halflife for a rat would be one-fourth this value or three hours. This represents sixteen halflifes of the drug or a final concentration of about 0.002% of its original concentration. A simple calculation will show that morphine is down to this level after 48 hours. This would indicate that heroin use every 48 hours should not lead to physical addiction. By and large, this is the case, but it is not always true.

There are many factors other than halflife, which may affect the onset of physical addiction. One is that, since purity levels are variable, users cannot administer the same amount of the drug each time. Even if this were the case, a heroin user is very unlikely to do the same amount each time, because of tolerance. Instead, he will increase his dosage. This will cause addiction to occur faster, just as reducing dosage each day will delay or even prevent addiction.

Another problem is that most people do not perceive 48 hours correctly. They would use at 6:00 p.m. and then again at 11:00 p.m. one night. Two days later they would use at 6:00 p.m. thinking that they were waiting 48 hours when, in fact, they had only waited 43 hours.

What the halflife of morphine means is that you cannot use it every other day and expect to avoid physical addiction. In general, it takes 48 hours for the morphine in your body to be reduced to a level that is truly negligible. If you are planning to use as much as possible without becoming addicted then you need to have two clean days for every day you use. I knew a woman who used every other day and she managed to develop a small addiction. The reason was simple: she did not wait 48 hours between usage. As discussed above, she miscalculated the number of hours so that most of the time it was only forty hours between usage.

I have heard all kinds of stuff about how hard it is to become addicted to heroin — how you have to use it daily for a month. This is complete hogwash, which probably dates back to the time when heroin purity was only 3% (it may have been true then). The amount of continuous use that one can do is dependent upon the user. It depends upon the speed of your metabolism, your exact usage patterns, and how sensitive you are to the withdrawal symptoms. Early on in my career, I used nightly for five consecutive days. This ended in a substantial number of withdrawal symptoms including violent diarrhea and sleeplessness for two days. Studies with morphine indicate that people show some withdrawal symptoms after being given morphine continuously for as few as three days.

Table 2: When these rules are followed religiously, it is almost impossible for a user to become addicted to heroin.

How to Stay Unaddicted
1. The number of consecutive days you use is always followed by twice that many days without using.
2. Never use more than three consecutive days.
3. Never use more than four times in a week.
4. Never use more than twelve times in a month.

Suppose that you wish to use as often as possible without becoming physically addicted: how often can you use? There are two rules, which will keep you safe from physical addiction if you follow them religiously. First, after a run of consecutive days in which you used, you must not use for twice as many days as you used. If you used two days in a row, for example, you must not use for the four days afterwards. You must be very careful about this. If you used Tuesday at 6:00 p.m. and then used Wednesday at 3:00 p.m., you used two consecutive days. Any time you used over more than a 12-hour period, you used two days in a row. The amount of clean time you need is measured in 24-hour intervals. So if you used two consecutive days, you should be clean for 96 hours. Don't play games with days.

The second rule for avoiding physical addiction is to never use more than three days in a row. But even after just three days, you may find that you have difficulty sleeping. One thing you will notice when you use three days in a row is that your tolerance goes way up — it may well take you ten times as much heroin to get high the third day as it did the first. As a result of this factor alone, you should avoid using consecutive days.

From these two rules, many other rules can be derived. Never use more than four times in a one-week period. Never use more than twelve times in a month.[3] In these two cases, remember that we are talking about periods. So a week is not Sunday through Saturday. There should be no seven-day period in which you use more than four times. Similarly, there should be no thirty-day period in which you use more than twelve times. There are several others that you will find if you play around with the rules and a calendar. The rules are summarized in Table 2.

These constitute rules that will normally keep you safe from physical addiction. During the end of my run as a chipper (after my run as an addict), I developed more strict rules, which provided much greater safety. It helps that they are also simpler: You may use over the course of one eight hour period in any three-day (72 hour) period. This means you can use during a small portion of one day and then you cannot use at all during the following two days.

This discussion should not give you the idea that you should use as often as possible. The less you use, the better off you will be. There are ill effects that stem from long-term intense chipping. These include an overall lowered energy level, irritability, insomnia, and psychological addiction. These are problems that manifest slowly, however. You may not even notice them until you stop using. Intense chipping can also affect your lifestyle. You may find that there is little in your life other than heroin and that you are spending a lot of money on heroin (when I quit chipping I was spending $300 per week on heroin — many addicts spend less than this). Basically, any problem that an addict has will also be experienced by an aggressive chipper. Try to always keep heroin as part of your life, but don't make it all of your life.

---

[3] Using four times in one week is done by using in the following order: use, clean, clean, use, use, use, clean. Note that almost the entire next week must be clean. Using twelve times in one month is done by using three days in a row after repeating the following sequence nine times: use, clean, clean.

Disease

I met a girl in court-mandated drug treatment who was addicted to Vicodin. When they finally arrested her, she was doing 40 pills per day. Vicodin has two active ingredients: hydrocodone (5 mg) and acetaminophen (500 mg). This means that every day she was ingesting 200 mg of hydrocodone and 20 grams (that's right, grams) of acetaminophen. She was arrested because of the hydrocodone she was taking — the acetaminophen is perfectly legal. And yet, the main damage that she was doing to her body was the result of the acetaminophen — the drug the government isn't trying to protect us all from. The hydrocodone is relatively harmless, while the acetaminophen is toxic to the liver.

This illustrates an important point about the diseases you expose yourself to as a heroin user: the heroin is rarely the problem. In fact, if you follow the procedures discussed in Chapter Three carefully, you don't need to worry about disease that much. But even under the best of circumstances, you still run a risk of acquiring all of them.

Curable Diseases

Most of the diseases that heroin users are prone to are curable. But left untreated, most of them will kill you. In the discussion below, refer to Figure 9 for the locations of the major organs.

Respiratory Depression

Respiratory depression is a direct effect of heroin itself: it slows down your breathing. Under most circumstances this is not a big problem. Your body is used to getting increasing or decreasing levels of oxygen at different times and, furthermore, your body does not use all of the oxygen that it inhales. In fact, the air that we all exhale still has a high percentage of oxygen in it. But one can be harmed by this effect.

The main negative effect of a true overdose of heroin is greatly reduced (often to none whatsoever) breathing. After roughly five minutes without oxygen, the brain will suffer serious and irreversible damage. After roughly ten minutes without oxygen, the body will die. The positive side of this is that a heroin overdose usually does not cause the user to simply stop breathing. Instead, his breathing is greatly slowed. Under these circumstances, it usually takes him about an hour to die. If he is with other people, there is usually plenty of time to get medical attention. This is one reason why people should not use heroin alone.

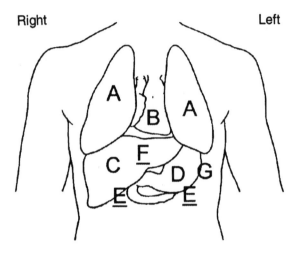

Figure 9
The main organs of the upper torso. Lungs (A), heart (B), liver (C),
stomach (D), kidneys (E), gallbladder (F), the pancreas and spleen (G).
The organs that are towards the back of the body are underlined.
Note that the rib cage ends at about the top of the stomach.

There are possible effects on the brain due to a minor decrease in respiration over long periods of time — that is, you get stupid. Your brain needs oxygen in order to work properly. Continued decreased levels of oxygen can have similar effects to having no oxygen at all for small periods of time. This is an issue that is more important to addicts than to chippers.

Endocarditis
When I was an addict, nothing scared me as much as endocarditis. AIDS and hepatitis didn't even come close. I thought that

endocarditis could kill me instantly and it didn't help matters that I knew that it was this thing growing on the valves of my heart; that's a pretty scary image. But like most junkies, my knowledge was not exactly accurate.

Endocarditis is an infection of the inner lining of the heart. At one time it was always fatal and you couldn't do anything about it — you still can't. Broadly speaking, there are two types: acute infectious endocarditis and subacute infectious endocarditis. What differentiates the two are the bacteria that cause them and the rate at which they progress. The subacute form is most common. It is caused by a streptococcus bacterium (the same thing that causes strep throat) called *streptococcus viridans*. If untreated, it will kill you within a year. The acute form of endocarditis is thankfully much less common. It is caused by a couple of different bacteria: *staphylococcus aureus* and *streptococcus hemolyticus*. It will kill you in about a month.

The bacteria get caught in the heart where they adhere to the inner lining known as the endocardium. Once there, they grow. These bacterial colonies become very large and pieces of them break off and enter the circulatory system. These bacterial "particles" then get trapped in various places in the body. In the brain, they can cause paralysis and brain abscesses; in the kidneys, they cause blood to appear in the urine; in the skin they cause the appearance of pinpoint-sized hemorrhages called petechiae.

These symptoms of the disease will give you some indication that you should see a doctor. The classic symptoms (someone with endocarditis may have none, some, or all of these) are: petechiae in the skin, blood in the urine, and a long-term low-grade fever. If you experience any of these symptoms, you should see a doctor.

The subacute form of endocarditis is mostly limited to people with existing heart problems. These may be congenital, due to previous rheumatic heart disease, or due to previous endocarditis. If you have had previous problems, you should be particularly careful and alert to symptoms.

The acute form of endocarditis is not linked with existing heart problems and it generally takes a very large infestation of bacteria to cause a problem. As always, clean needle technique is key to avoiding problems.

Antibiotic treatment is usually quite successful in treating subacute infectious endocarditis. The sooner such treatment starts, the better off you will be; it is still possible to die from this if treatment is started too late. Acute infectious endocarditis progresses so rapidly that antibiotic treatment usually must be combined with surgery. Even with this, life is generally only prolonged. The trauma to the heart usually ends up shortening the sufferer's life considerably.

Pulmonary Edema

Pulmonary edema is the swelling of lung tissue. The main result of this is to reduce the lung capacity, usually to about 50% of its full capacity. It can lead to very potent pneumonia, which can lead to death. Generally, this is a problem associated with overdose. It appears to be linked with existing lung disease, but whether this is due to heroin, adulterants, or other causes (e.g., cigarettes) is unclear.

Blood Clots

A thrombus is a blood clot. Primarily, they form in veins because blood moves more slowly in veins than in arteries. The clotting process is started by the platelets in the blood. In order to do this, the platelets need to adhere to some surface. Under most circumstances, the walls of the veins are too smooth to allow the process to begin. But injection scars inside of veins create excellent surfaces for the platelets to adhere to and begin the clotting process. To reduce the risk of clotting, exercise — paying particular attention to parts of your body in which you inject.

These clots may stick in the walls of the arteries and form hard clumps that interfere with the flow of blood. These are fairly common among injectors. They are usually frightening at first, but over time users find that they aren't particularly painful and that they don't seem to cause any problems other than making the vein in which they reside useless for injection. Veins that are constricted in this way will divert blood to other veins. Under most circumstances, this is not a big problem but if too much constriction exists in an arm or leg, the limb may slowly suffocate.

Blood clots in other areas of the body produce effects similar to endocarditis, discussed above. Of particular concern is clotting in the lungs. This can cause chest pain, coughing, and shortness of breath.

High Blood Pressure

All of the garbage that gets introduced into the body as a result of the ingestion of impure heroin can cause many different problems. These foreign substances can react not only with each other, but also with normal parts of the body to produce particulate matter. Over time, this material will be removed from your body. But until then, it can often be found floating through your blood stream. The presence of this material constricts the flow of blood — leading to high blood pressure.

High blood pressure puts an extra strain on the blood vessels. This causes them to lose their elasticity; they become hard. As a result of this, the arteries become narrower, which increases the blood pressure even more. This high blood pressure creates a greater strain on the heart as it pumps blood through the body. The overworked heart then becomes prone to heart disease.

This situation is particularly bad for junkies. First, junkies do not stop using long enough for their bodies to recover and expel the foreign substances. Second, almost all junkies smoke cigarettes. Third, most junkies do not eat well — the number one junkie food is high in fat: pizza. Infrequent chippers should not have to worry so much about high blood pressure. Regardless, all heroin users should check their blood pressure often — I recommend once a week.

Liver Damage

The liver can be infected due to viruses introduced in the administration process. Life is not possible without the liver. It is the primary means by which your body removes toxins. Many drugs heavily strain the liver; but heroin does not. But remember: unclean administration can introduce any number of viruses, which can attack the liver.

Tetanus

Most people grow up thinking of tetanus as a joke disease that has something to do with rust. In fact, tetanus comes from the tetanus bacillus that lives in the intestines of all animals (including you). It is excreted in fecal matter and can live in soil indefinitely. For obvious reasons, it is most commonly found in manure. It lives in dead tissue (like skin) and does not cause local inflammation — this is one reason why it is such a dangerous disease: you often won't know that you have it until it is too late.

The tetanus bacillus creates a toxin, which passes to the central nervous system. This toxin causes the nervous system to misbehave — telling muscles to stiffen and often causing painful spasms and convulsions. The first muscles affected are usually the jaws, which explains why tetanus is often referred to as "Lock Jaw." If the respirator muscles are affected, asphyxiation can occur. This point cannot be stressed enough: tetanus from even a very small wound can kill you. Stay current on your tetanus shots.

Abscesses

An abscess is a collection of pus in a cavity. Skin abscesses are usually caused by *staphylococcus aureus* — the very stuff that will kill you if you get enough of it into your heart. Normally, the core of the abscess dies and liquefies. This is the pus. For heroin users, abscesses are most often just the sign of a subcutaneous injection (often unintentional). Although often painful, abscesses are not a major health concern except when they get infected.

If you get an abscess, soak it in hot water. This will relieve some of the pain that the abscess causes, in addition to healing it more quickly. If an abscess remains for more than a couple of days, you should have a doctor look at it. An infected abscess is a very serious problem and can cause the loss of limbs or even death in extreme circumstances.

Bacteria

In the process of ingesting heroin, you ingest countless bacteria. Most of these are not of much concern — you ingest many just breathing. The means of ingesting heroin, however, are more invasive than breathing; that is, there are fewer mechanisms for filtering out the bacteria. There are many bacteria, which can greatly harm your body. It is impossible to discuss all of them here (medical science hasn't even identified all of them), but this fact should be further encouragement to keep your ingestion technique as clean as possible.

Pupil Constriction

Heroin causes the constriction of the pupils in the eyes. As a result of this, it can be very hard to see at night. This problem is greatly multiplied by the use of quinine as an adulterant in heroin (almost exclusively white powder heroin). Quinine is a tissue poison affecting the brain, heart, muscles, kidneys, blood, ears, and eyes. Mild doses of it produce ringing in the ears, headache, nausea, and decreased vision. Moderate amounts of it produce deafness, vomiting, diarrhea, blindness, confusion, delirium, and even death due to respiratory arrest. The primary side effect is decreased vision. This is only temporary, but you should be careful — particularly at night.

Nerve Damage

Nerve damage to the skin is a common problem stemming from repeated injections into an area of skin. Depending upon the extent of damage, it may never be repaired. This will cause parts of the skin to be numb. The numbness usually coexists with injection scars.

Menstrual Cycle Disruption

Heroin also affects women in particular, by disrupting the menstrual cycle. It does so by affecting the pituitary gland and the hypothalamus. The pituitary gland releases a hormone that is related to ovulation. This problem goes away when the woman stops using. Women wishing to get pregnant should avoid using heroin for this as well as other reasons.

All of the diseases discussed above affect users who inject, but in some cases they affect smokers and snorters, too (see Table 3). There are diseases which are specific to smokers and snorters. Mostly, the negative effects of overuse of heroin by smoking or snorting are rare, however, because users prone to this will most likely switch to injection as their primary route of administration.

Table 3: Health risks of special concern to heroin users. Severity is "great" (G), "moderate" (M), or "small" (S). Some of the risks are associated with all (All) methods of administration and some are only associated with injection (Inj).

Problem	Severity	Method
AIDS	G	Inj
Hepatitis	G	All
Respiratory Depression	M	All
Endocarditis	G	Inj
Pulmonary Edema	M	All
Thrombus (Lungs)	M	Inj
Thrombus (Skin)	S	Inj
High Blood Pressure	M	Inj
Liver Disease	M	All
Tetanus	G	Inj
Skin Abscesses	S	Inj
Bacteria in Blood	S to G	All
Vision Problems	S	All
Skin Numbness	S	Inj
Menstruation Disruption	S	All

Smoking Problems

Cigarettes are damaging to the human body for a lot more reasons than the nicotine that is ingested. Smoking any substance involves bombarding the lungs with hot particulate matter. No part of the body likes to be bombarded with hot particulate matter, but the lungs are a particularly sensitive organ. Everything bad that you've heard about smoking cigarettes applies to smoking heroin. The only thing that may make smoking heroin less damaging is that you are quite likely to smoke a smaller amount of heroin as compared to the amount of tobacco a typical cigarette smoker smokes.

Snorting Problems

Excessive snorting of foreign substances can cause ulceration of the mucus membrane of the nose. In extreme cases, a hole will be eaten through the nasal septum — the wall that separates one side of your nose from the other.

The ABCs of Hepatitis

You can get hepatitis from ingesting heroin via any method of administration, but it is most likely with snorting since the heroin is never cooked. Hepatitis has a strong association with injection because of unhygienic procedures. Regardless of the method of administration, when you keep company with heroin users, you risk infection of hepatitis. Although it may not seem possible, a sneeze or a cough can propel particles ten or more feet from the location of the ejection. These particles can land on syringes or other implements, thereby running the risk of being transported into your body.

Hepatitis is the inflammation of the liver. There are numerous forms of this disease, but three are primary: A, B, and C. Each is caused by a distinct virus. I will discuss each form of hepatitis below, but first we must discuss the liver and its importance to life.

The liver is a regenerative organ. It has three primary functions: modulation of blood sugar (energy) levels; creation of bile; and removal of poisons. The liver gets blood from two sources: oxygenated blood from the hepatic artery and nutrient rich blood from the portal vein, which comes from the stomach, intestines, spleen, and pancreas. The blood from the small intestines carries absorbed nutrients such as sugars and amino acids. When there is an excess of these nutrients, the liver stores them. When there is a deficiency, the liver releases them. In this way, the liver modulates the blood sugar levels so that they never get too high or too low. The liver also secretes bile. Bile is the substance in the body that breaks fat down to sugar so that the body can use it.

Probably the most important function of the liver is removing poisons from the body. This is critical to the body's ability to heal itself. Most drugs are seen by the liver as poisons, so excessive drug use can greatly tax the liver. Alcohol is particularly associated with liver damage. In fact, alcohol abuse is the number one cause of cirrhosis of the liver.

Cirrhosis of the liver is the chronic destruction of its cells. A cirrhotic liver loses its organization, which is critical to this complex organ. As a result of this, the liver stops functioning. When the liver cells are damaged, they are replaced by scar tissue. This tissue has none of the liver cell functions. In effect, that part of the liver is no longer liver. When cirrhosis of the liver begins, it causes the liver to be enlarged because of the regenerative process that is happening. But later, the liver shrinks because of the contraction of the scar tissue.

Hepatitis A is the least serious form of hepatitis. It usually comes from contaminated water or food and spreads under conditions of poor sanitation. The incubation period is two to six weeks. Its symptoms include: loss of appetite, nausea, mild fever, darkness of urine, and sometimes jaundice (yellowish pigmentation of the skin). In general, the liver will be enlarged but no permanent liver damage results.

Hepatitis B is much more serious than type A. It can lead to chronic (long-term) hepatitis or cirrhosis of the liver. Hepatitis B is generally transmitted via blood — shared or dirty syringes and unprotected sex. The symptoms for type B are about the same as for type A, but the onset is slower: it generally takes two to six months for type B symptoms to appear. The severity of the disease depends largely on the physical health of the sufferer before the disease took effect. This is why hepatitis can be particularly hard on junkies.

Hepatitis C is quite similar to type B. There are only a few differences. The incubation period is highly variable. Generally, it is anywhere from two weeks to six months. But increasingly, the disease seems able to stay dormant for many years. There is currently no cure for hepatitis C.

AIDS

For anyone who doesn't know this: AIDS is an acronym for Acquired Immunodeficiency Syndrome. It is believed to be caused by HIV, which is another acronym for Human Immunodeficiency Virus. AIDS destroys your immune system. This makes you very susceptible to infection. This is because HIV invades your white blood cells and destroys their ability to fight infection.

HIV is a retrovirus, which means that it carries its genetic information via RNA instead of DNA. What does this mean to you? Nothing — nothing at all. What matters is this: if you get AIDS, you will die within about a decade. Once infected with HIV, it will lay dormant for two to eight years. Once symptoms develop, you are said to have AIDS. The symptoms are: weight loss, enlarged lymph nodes, diarrhea, fever, and night sweats.

If you experience any of the symptoms of AIDS you should, of course, see a doctor. But generally, a doctor will not be able to do much for you if you have full-blown AIDS. For this reason, you should get tested for HIV infection as often as is reasonable. This means every six months if you are involved in dangerous activities such as sharing needles or having unprotected sex. If you are living a reasonably clean life, then you should test for HIV every two years — if you're doing heroin, you aren't living *that* clean a life.

Various drugs and therapies can prolong the life of a person infected with HIV. But, by far, the best thing you can do for yourself is to get healthy. Your first reaction to finding out you are infected will likely be to submerge yourself in heroin. But this will only put added pressure on your body and cause you to have a shorter, and more importantly, a sicker life. Try to look on the bright side: you might live longer with AIDS alone than you would have with heroin alone.

Go To the Doctor

Other than AIDS and Hepatitis C, every problem related to heroin is curable. So when you notice that something is not right with your body, you should go to the doctor.

While reading this section, you may have noticed that the symptoms of the various diseases are very similar. A fever may be caused by something as benign as a blood clot or as devastating as AIDS. It is important to remember that the normal symptoms of a particular disease will not always appear in all sufferers. As a result of this fact, don't think that simply because you don't have pinpoint-sized hemorrhages on your skin (but you do have blood in your urine) that you aren't suffering from endocarditis. Go to the doctor; a simple blood test will usually determine the problem. Sometimes a little pressing and prodding by the doctor will do the same. You should look out for the symptoms in Table 4.

Table 4: Symptoms of diseases that are of special concern to heroin users.

Symptoms	Lifestyle?
Long-term Fever	no
Blood in Urine	no
Paralysis	no
Abscesses	yes
Petechiae	no
Difficulty Breathing	no
High Blood Pressure	no
Uncontrollable Muscle Tightness	no
Vomiting	yes
Diarrhea	yes
Weight Loss	no

Many heroin users are afraid to talk to a doctor about their medical problems. This is understandable because many doctors are anything but understanding about the problems that illegal drug users face. One female junkie I talked to was told by a physician: "Of course you're sick; you're a junkie! What do you want me to do about it?" Her answer was to slink away, basically getting no medical treatment.

My response (and I hope yours from now on) is: "Act like a professional." Regardless of whether you are the most infrequent chipper or the most messed-up junkie, you are still a human being and you deserve to be treated with the compassion and dignity that should always exist between a doctor and his patient. Many doctors would have you believe otherwise, but when they are seeing you, the relationship is employer to employee and you are the employer. It doesn't matter if you are paying for the visit or the government is paying for you — if you aren't there, the doctor doesn't get paid. I have found that doctors fall in line quickly once they see that you will not be intimidated.

You should not, however, go to the doctor with an attitude. There are plenty of doctors who are very kind and understanding about drug use. In fact, medicine has a higher percentage of junkies in it than any other profession. If you're lucky, you'll get a junkie doctor.[4] Junkies you meet will often know of a doctor who is sympathetic to the problems of drug users. Ask around — it can't hurt. One thing that no doctor likes, however, is to be treated as a drug dealer. There are times when you can reasonably get some pharmaceuticals from your doctor, but when you come in concerned about an ailment is not one of them.

You should be honest with your doctor. Tell him why you think there may be a problem. Have you shared syringes? Reused syringes? Used around sick people? In dirty places? Tell him whatever you think is relevant. This, in itself, will be an invitation to the physician to be professional and helpful.

On the other hand, if you use heroin very infrequently or you do not inject, the physician will not be able to tell that you are a drug user. Every disease that is associated with heroin use can be caught in other ways.

You may want to keep any drug-related ailments off your official medical records. You can do this by hiring a private physician (out of town if you live in a small town) and paying cash. If it turns out that you have something that is serious, such as AIDS, your detection as a drug user may be less important to you and may convince you to see your regular doctor.

You can also dress down and go to a free inner-city clinic. There are problems associated with this, however. First, it may take you all day to see someone. Second, you will probably need some kind of identification in order to get treated for anything but an emergency. In this case, you may want to look into getting a fake ID.

---

[4] Several studies have shown that junkie (usually morphine-addicted) doctors are just as good at their jobs as their non-addicted colleagues.

Overdose

When a heroin user dies with a needle still stuck in his arm, the death is usually written off as an overdose without much more thought given to it. This is unfortunate because most deaths attributed to heroin overdose are simply not overdoses of heroin. Ignorance of this causes unnecessary deaths among addicts and chippers alike.

From 1940 to 1970 the percentage of deaths among addicts attributed to overdose in New York City grew steadily from roughly zero to 80%. During this time, the addict population stayed more or less the same size, as indicated by deaths due to other causes such as suicide. This data is indicative of one thing: most deaths attributed to heroin overdose are caused by something else.

The reasons that these deaths are commonly attributed to heroin overdose stem from the professional lives of medical examiners. The job of a medical examiner is not easy. It is often very difficult to determine the cause of death of a body. This problem is exacerbated when the body suffers from many ailments, as is the case with most addicts. Around 1940 it became the fashion in the industry to label all deaths among heroin addicts as overdose if no other cause of death could be determined.

The determination of death by overdose of heroin rested on two findings. First, the patient must have been an injecting heroin user. Second, the patient must have shown no signs of death by suicide, violence, or natural causes. Medical examiners were not expected to even do blood tests to show that a high concentration of heroin or morphine was present. This is still largely the case today.

Death due to overdose is a slow process which ends in respiratory failure. Under most circumstances, it takes at least an hour for someone to die of an overdose. The user basically passes out and gradually gets less and less oxygen, to the point of death. I have been around various people who have died for short periods of time,[5] and in none of the cases did this kind of gradual process take place. In each case, the victim died quite suddenly indicating that it was not a true overdose.

It is very hard to overdose on opioids. Lawrence Kolb and A.G. Du Mez did the only really relevant study on this issue back in 1931. They worked with non-addicted monkeys and gave them IV injections of heroin. They found that it takes at least 7 milligrams of heroin per kilogram of body weight to overdose a monkey. In the following equation, H_{od} is the number of milligrams of heroin necessary to overdose a person with a weight of W pounds.

$$H_{od} = 7 \times W / 2.2$$

Let's look at what this formula means. A kilogram is 2.2 pounds so you can determine your weight in kilograms by dividing your weight in pounds by 2.2. I weigh 120 pounds, so my weight is 120 / 2.2 or 55 kilograms. In order to find out what a lethal dose of heroin would be for me, I multiply the number of kilograms I weigh by 7 milligrams. 55 x 7 = 385 milligrams. Note three things about this number. First, this is pure heroin — it isn't cut with anything. Today, this would represent about a gram of street heroin. In 1970, this would have represented almost 13 grams!

The second important thing about this number is that it represents a single injection. This is the amount of heroin needed to overdose a person at one injection. It is fairly common for a user to ingest a gram of heroin over the course of an evening (although this is quite a lot — the user would have to be fairly wealthy). But it is quite hard to ingest a gram of heroin in a single administration. Administering 13 grams in such a manner is a practical impossibility.

The third issue is that addicts (and most of the deaths were of addicts) have a tolerance to the drug. I've discussed how tolerance is bad in that it requires more and more heroin in order to get you high. But it is also good in that it makes death by overdose less likely.

---

[5] In all cases, medical professionals were called or first aid was performed by those present, and the victim survived.

This discussion should not lead you to think that it is impossible to overdose on heroin. Sometimes you will get heroin that is basically pure — this may lead to an overdose. Another potential problem is that your environment will affect the way you react to a dose of heroin (or any drug for that matter). If you are used to using at home and you use at a friend's house, your tolerance may go down and you may overdose. You can avoid these problems by being moderate in your intake of heroin. Also, if you only use when others are around, you will most likely reduce the risk of an overdose.

The cases that are generally referred to as overdoses — but which are not — have two distinct characteristics: they are sudden and accompanied by pulmonary edema (swelling of lung tissue). Most cases were also characterized by the accumulation of fluid in the brain and the fragmentation of astrocytes in the brain.

What exactly is killing the heroin addicts is unclear, but it seems to be drug interactions. There is some indication that quinine, which is commonly used to cut white powder heroin, interacts with the heroin to cause lethal results. Quinine overdose all by itself causes the same kind of death as is seen in the sudden deaths associated with heroin. The good news about this is that the current high purity heroin available makes this kind of overdose less common (although it makes real overdoses more common).

A second possible cause is what I call the Janis Joplin Effect: the combining of heroin with central nervous system depressants such as alcohol and barbiturates. Ms. Joplin comes home after a hard night of drinking — a successful night you might say, since she is hammered, pissed, drunk, blotto, whatever. As *Time* pointed out, "She apparently filled a hypodermic needle with heroin and shot it into her left arm. The injection killed her." It appears that this is incorrect. Had she not been drinking, Joplin would almost certainly not have died that night.

The combination of low doses of morphine with high blood alcohol levels has long been known to cause fatalities. This is almost certainly what happened to Janis Joplin. The particularly bad aspect of this is that users often take "downers" to intensify the effect of heroin when only a small amount is administered or the quality is poor. Make no mistake, this will kill you. Heroin interacts very poorly with alcohol and other central nervous system depressants.

Generally, this effect is brought about by high alcohol (or other drug) levels along with moderate or even small heroin levels. This, of course, goes against "common sense." I know of a case where an ex-junkie wanted to use heroin but he was afraid of becoming readdicted. So he went about using in the safest way he could think of: he got drunk so that he wouldn't have to use much heroin to feel it. He used only a small amount of heroin and then only smoked it. The result: he died.

Never use heroin with alcohol or barbiturates. I don't care if you don't feel drunk. Don't do it. I've personally been witness to too many deaths due to the Janis Joplin Effect. If you want to kill yourself, fine. My only advice is to do it by yourself so that no one has to bother with you until you're good and dead. But if you still have some wish to continue living, don't mix these drugs.

This brings up another mixture of drugs: the speedball. A speedball is heroin mixed with cocaine. Although this is a dangerous drug combination, it does not seem to lead to death anymore than cocaine alone. In other words, heroin and cocaine do not appear to interact poorly. For more information on cocaine, I recommend the *Cocaine Handbook*, listed in Appendix B.

Final Thoughts

Doing any drug is dangerous. But with heroin, there are two things that you can do that eliminate 99% of the risks: don't inject and don't mix drugs. This still means that you can end up addicted to heroin. But addiction by itself is not going to kill you. With a little care, you can remain alive and unaddicted as a heroin user.

Chapter Five
Legal Issues

This is the part of the book that makes me most angry. Even most of the health-related problems associated with heroin use are caused by the fact that heroin is illegal. And the remaining risks are at least exacerbated by the laws. My direct run-ins with the law were always made worse by my certainty that the enforcement of vice laws were nothing more than an elaborate game designed to punish those members of society who had the gall to pursue their happiness based upon their own desires and not those of society.

It frustrates me greatly that some people spend half their lives in jail because their drug of choice differs from the drug of choice of the majority of society. Make no mistake: as a heroin user, you suffer from political oppression. You suffer from it in the poor and variable quality of heroin you buy. You suffer from it in the high price you pay for heroin. And most of all, you suffer from it when you are arrested and incarcerated. Nineteenth Century England had the homosexuals, Hitler and Stalin had the Jews, Pol Pot had the intellectuals, and the United States has the drug users.

But these political concerns are the business of people who don't use heroin. Your concern is to stay hidden and not be noticed by law enforcement. If you are noticed, your concern will be to extricate yourself from the legal system as quickly as possible. I wish I could just tell you to move to another country. This worked well, when possible, for the homosexuals, Jews, and intellectuals.

But unfortunately, the United States is so powerful that it has managed to export its oppression of drug users into most other countries of the world. There are indications that this is slowly changing, but the situation is still bleak.

Not Getting Arrested

The best way to deal with the legal system is to never get caught. So before I talk about how best to deal with the various aspects of the system, I want to talk about what you can do to minimize your risk of being caught in the first place.

Drug Deals

I have already addressed this subject in Chapter Two because your biggest risk from law enforcement will come from acquiring heroin. Follow the suggestions in that chapter, but let me add a little to it here.

Do not score on the street any more often than you have to. Get a pager number as quickly as possible. It is relatively easy for a cop to spot a street dealer. Usually, buyers are only arrested in order to get evidence of a drug sale — in other words, you're a small fish. But you'll be arrested and prosecuted just the same. So limit the amount of time you spend acquiring from street dealers.

Despite what you've seen on cop shows, it is very hard to tail a car, especially without being noticed. So if you can do a deal in a car, you are at an advantage. Try this: have the dealer pick you up at a public place, but choose different places each time. Drive away with the dealer and do the deal after a few minutes. Have the dealer drop you off somewhere other than where you were picked up.

Heroin is often sold in balloons. If it is, you have the option of transporting it in your mouth. Should police arrive, you can swallow the evidence without losing it — you will excrete it later or you can even force yourself to vomit it up if not much time has passed. I was never willing to store heroin in my mouth because I was always afraid of the diseases that my dealers were carrying.

Whether or not you do this depends upon your tolerance for this kind of risk as opposed to legal risk.

Having dealers come to your home is relatively risk-free if they only come by once a week or so. Otherwise, your neighbors will probably notice them, especially if the dealer is of an ethnic difference from that of the neighborhood. Take great care in doing drug deals at your home.

Medical Emergencies

The only other real legal risk you run is when you or someone you are with has a drug-related medical emergency, which requires paramedic assistance. Cops are always taught to make sure that they try to save the life of an overdose victim rather than worrying about an arrest. Many cops, despite this training, will go through a user's belongings looking for "evidence" while the paramedics save the user's life. In these cases, the user often ends up with a ride to the hospital *and* a citation for a felony. If you are around a user who experiences a medical problem, see to his physical safety first. After that, see to his overall safety — and yours — by removing any incriminating evidence from the area. You can limit problems in this area by using within a group. In that case, a couple of people can administer first aid to the user, another can call 911, and another can "clean up."

Dealing With Police

How do I put this gently? Cops are not the brightest lights in the house and their lack of knowledge could act as a damning indictment of our educational system. Let me give you an example. A cop was looking at some mail that I had, because he thought that I was stealing someone else's mail. For some reason, the addressee had been scratched off the mail — so he could not prove his suspicion. But he found, on one of the pieces of mail, the following line, "Courtesy of Jim Witless." The cop thought he had me. He grabbed me by the shoulder with great anger and said, "Jim Witless! Is that your name?! What are you doing with other people's mail?" I responded with complete exasperation, "That means it *came* from Jim Witless, not that it was *sent* to Jim Witless." I was arrested right then because the cop didn't know what "courtesy of" meant (ignorance) and was unwilling to find out what it meant (stupidity).

I have known cops as a junkie, an ordinary law-abiding citizen, and even as a personal acquaintance. As a result, I can say with some assurance that, with notable exceptions, cops do not enter law enforcement for noble reasons. Mostly, they fall into the job. But they stay because it works for them — they like the job. And given that 90% of the laws they enforce are unethical (consensual crimes against "morality" or "good sense"), you know they're not in it because they want to make society a better place. A recent article by a vice cop in *The New Yorker* said that he thought the whole process of arresting users and dealers was just a game: the good guys versus the bad guys.

Police Personalities

Understanding the psychology of police officers is very useful. It will certainly make dealing with them more pleasant and will greatly increase your chances of talking your way out of difficult situations. Long before I ever even tried heroin, I was terribly afraid of cops. I wondered why it was that when I got pulled over by a cop for forgetting to use my turn signal, I would end up with a ticket while people I knew would get off with a warning after tailgating a cop at 80 mph in their marijuana-smoke-filled cars. Eventually, I found out and in retrospect, it was pretty obvious: from the officer's perspective, I was not *us*, I was *them*. They don't like giving out tickets to people who could be their friends. They don't mind doing so to people with whom they share no connection. In fact, they often relish giving these people tickets.

Psychological Types

I will talk about police psychology from two perspectives. First, I will discuss personality types and show you what this means in terms of how cops think and perceive. Second, I will talk about the sociology of cops and how they perceive themselves. The first issue will allow you to get inside the head of a cop (don't worry — there's plenty of room!) and understand how you need to talk in order to communicate with him in terms that he will understand. The second issue will allow you to better manipulate the cop so that he will like you more and thus be more inclined to let you go.

Well over a half century ago, Carl Jung published a book called *Psychological Types.* In this book, he argued that there are four key attributes of personality with which people are born. Everyone is oriented one way or the other with regard to these attributes. He also noted that there is nothing good or bad about being oriented any which way but that there is a tendency to attribute moral weakness and even insanity to those who are oriented differently from ourselves.

A key element of Jung's theory and undoubtedly the reason it is so popular in our "do you own thing" and "no-fault" society is that it allows people to be different without the need to be fixed (unless, of course, they're illegal drug users). But even those who understand the theory still succumb to the temptation to consider other types inferior. I know that I do. For example, I was very pleased to see that my personality type was very under-represented on the police force. "Of course," I thought, "people as smart and kind and good looking as me just don't become cops." But from a practical standpoint, this fact explains why my interactions with cops, even under the best of circumstances, have been strained.

There are four elements of the theory of personality types. The first element is the attitude. This may be divided into either introversion or extroversion. This is the most fundamental element of personality. It determines whether one's primary focus comes from external phenomena or internal perceptions. Generally, introverts are thought to be shy. While this is often the case, it is not always so.

The second element is the judgment function, which is either thinking or feeling. Thinking types tend to place themselves outside of any situation or concept that they are thinking about. As a result, they can be quite objective but also can be perceived as somewhat heartless. Feeling types place themselves in the middle of whatever they are thinking about. They tend to generate more subjective logic, but it is a logic that is more understanding of humans and human frailty.

A good illustration of this second element comes from the movie *Seven Beauties*. In it, the main character is in a Nazi concentration camp. He is forced to select eight prisoners who will be put to death. If he does not do so, all of the prisoners will be killed. This bothers the main character greatly but, being a thinking type, he has no trouble stepping outside the situation and making the choice — if he makes no choice, they all die. Another character thinks that this is madness and counsels him that they should not accept this deal. He says it is better that they all die together. This is a feeling character — his logic stems from placing himself in the position of being one of the eight to be killed.

The third element is perception, which is either sensation or intuition. According to Jung, sensation types perceive from their five senses, but intuition types perceive from their "sixth" sense. I don't accept this notion. I think that intuition types are more focused on subtleties when perceiving things. They often miss obvious things and note very elusive things.

The fourth element of the theory determines whether a person is oriented towards their judgment functions (called "rational" types) or their perception functions (called "irrational" types). There has been much confusion about this element of the theory since Jung's time. In particular, there is a notion that introverts exhibit the latter function. So if an introvert seems like a rational type he is really irrational. This aspect of the theory is highly conjectural. It doesn't really affect us in this discussion, but if you read more about this subject matter you may want to bear it in mind.

Given the idea that there are four elements to anyone's personality and that any one of those elements can be subdivided in one of two ways, there must be sixteen different personality types. Some of these types are very rare, occurring in less than 1% of all people. As a result of this, when studies are done on groups of people, a concept known as "temperament" is used. The temperament is the combination of the two functions. There are four temperaments: sensory-thinking (ST), intuitive-thinking (NT),[1] sensory-feeling (SF), and intuitive-feeling (NF). The percentage of

---

[1] "I" is not used for "intuitive" because it is reserved for the first elemental groups ("introverted").

police officers, as well as the general population, who are of the different temperaments are given in the Table 5.

Table 5: Temperaments of police.

Type	Police Officers	General Population
ST	64%	25%
NT	16%	18%
SF	14%	29%
NF	06%	28%

One thing is very clear from this chart: there are a hell of a lot of ST types on the police force. If you are this type, you should count your blessings because you should have a fairly easy time communicating with cops. But for the rest of us, it will take work to overcome our irrational mistrust of cops[2] and learn to communicate with them.

Table 6 provides a list of personality traits, which the different temperaments possess (this table is based upon *Thinking Cop/Feeling Cop*). This will give you a good idea of temperament most cops exhibit as well as a fairly good idea of what temperaments you exhibit.

Eighty percent of all cops are thinking oriented. This means that the vast majority of cops are not going to cut you any slack because you're in a bad place. By and large they don't care; you got yourself into this mess by doing illegal drugs (or whatever), and now you're going to pay the price.

Roughly 80% of all cops are also sensory oriented. This means that they base their decisions on what they see and not on hunches. This can be helpful or harmful. On the plus side, if there is no concrete physical evidence of a crime, you are likely to be able to talk your way out of whatever situation you are in because the cop will not press the issue. On the other side, cops are often keen observers; if there is anything incriminating to notice, they will likely notice it.

---

[2] This is in addition to our rational mistrust of cops — they *are* out to get us and they will often use unethical means to do so.

Table 6: Personality traits of the different temperaments.

ST	NT	SF	NF
Concrete	Precise	Sociable	Global
Decisive	Logical	Practical	Creative
Practical	Decisive	Loyal	Intense
Pragmatic	Conceptual	Structured	Perceptive
Direct	Cognitive	Traditional	Conceptual
Logical	Global	Caring	Gentle
Thorough	Factual	Organized	Idealistic
Impersonal	Strategic	Trusting	Devoted
Factual	Visionary	Thorough	Friendly
Analytical	Theoretical	Observant	Congenial
Traditional	Goal-Oriented	Considerate	Compassionate
Observant	Detached	Friendly	Committed
Sensible	Demanding	Tactful	Empathetic
Structured	Reserved	Cooperative	Diplomatic
Service Oriented	Charismatic	Concrete	Charismatic

Unless there is some compelling reason to think otherwise, you should assume that any cop you deal with is an ST. If you talk to him like an NF, he will think that you're odd at best, and at worst, that you're probably hiding something — and most likely you are. So don't talk to him about how painful your life is — save this for your NF social worker. Instead, talk in clear and concrete terms about what you are doing and what you have been doing. Don't mention people because cops don't mention people when they talk about their own lives. If you didn't know what a cop's job involved, you would think it was very much like being a gas meter reader from the descriptions of ST cops — you would never guess that their main function is working with people.

Police Self-Images

James M. Eagan, formerly of the New York State Police, has written a very informative book on avoiding speeding tickets. The best part of the book is that he gives great insight into the motivations of cops. He states that if an officer "doesn't possess the standard police issue personality on the day he is sworn in, he will soon." This is due to the sociology of police departments and the requirements of the job. According to Eagan, there are two emotions that control an officer's life: fear and an ego that can scarcely fit inside the borders of Montana.

The information system inside police forces act to constantly remind officers of the dangers of their jobs. Anytime a cop is injured, the information spreads to all the other officers in the organization. So cops get the impression that people are out to get them — and they are.[3]

The ego is represented in a cop's belief that he is "the man" (and it doesn't matter if he is a woman). This causes cops to always have an attitude and to insist upon having control of any situation.

Interacting with Police

In order to have a good relationship with a cop, you have to do two things: reduce his fear and stroke his ego. But these, and particularly the second, cannot be done in an obvious way. Cops may not be rocket scientists (or even accountants), but they aren't so stupid as to fall for obvious flattery. Remember that most cops are ST types and they are, thus, observant.

The first and most important thing you can do to reduce a cop's fear is to remain stationary. If you move, do so slowly and if you need to get anything out of your pockets, tell the officer first. (Example: "I'm going to get my wallet out of my back pocket.") I had a terrible time with cops when I first starting having impromptu meetings with them. One reason was that I always kept my wallet in the breast pocket of my jacket. The cop would say, "Can I see some identification?" I would tell him yes and reach for my breast pocket. Within about a minute I was in handcuffs. What I should

---

[3] Cab drivers and workers in a number of other occupations are more likely to get killed at work than cops are. But the point here is not the truth of the matter, but rather cops' perceptions of the matter. Concern for their physical safety is a primary motivation of most cops.

have done was to point to my breast pocket and say, "I keep my wallet in here." Then I should have unzipped my jacket, pulled the flap back, and reached very gingerly into the pocket and removed the wallet. Remember: cops will often use a sudden move for a wallet as cause for searching you, which may land you in jail when you could have gotten off free.

Overall, try to communicate with the officer as if he were a regular person. Smile at appropriate times (but not all the time or he'll think something's amiss). Make eye contact and try not to be self-effacing. In general, try to be an ST. You might even practice this. Look at the table of personality traits and improvise.

Eagan mentions a really obvious way in which people try to boost the ego of cops: they call the cop "sir" at every possible opportunity. Cops want you to respect them but they want to think that you mean it and that you aren't just doing it to get out of trouble. Eagan says to think of wolf packs. There is always a top dog in any wolf pack and when dealing with police, the top dog is the cop. You want to show him that you know he's the top dog in a million different subtle ways.

How do you show the cop that you think he is the top dog without lying on your back and offering your throat to him? The first and most important thing to do is to lose the attitude that I most obviously had. You need to love your local law enforcement. They're just here to make us safer and happier and healthier. Maybe I'm laying it on thick, but if you have an attitude about cops, you will be saying "fuck you" in a million subtle ways and you do not want this.

There are many little things you can do. If you are wearing sunglasses, you can take them off — even if the cop leaves his on. You can ask permission before doing something that might upset the cop, like moving. Going back to some things we discussed above: move slowly, make eye contact, smile.

Remain Silent

If you are having some kind of conflict with a cop, you must be careful that in trying to talk yourself out of trouble you don't talk yourself into trouble. This is something I learned collecting air samples in other countries. Whenever going through customs, the officials would always be concerned because the gas canisters looked a lot like bombs. Over time I realized that the less I talked, the fewer questions they asked. If you can answer a question with a simple "yes" or "no," then do so. The more details you add to your story (even if it's true), the more you open it up to examination and the more likely it is to "smell fishy." Keep your stories simple and direct.

The fact that I've given you a lot of information about how to communicate with cops should not be taken as a suggestion to not talk to them at all. It depends upon the situation. If a cop pulls you over for speeding or knocks on your door because your party has gone a little late, it is usually a good idea to talk. But if you try to score some heroin from an undercover cop, talking is only going to get you in more trouble. Remember two things: you really do have the right to remain silent (so far) and nothing you say is going to help you — in fact, it could hurt you.

Don't give away any of your rights. Don't allow a cop to search you. He may do so anyway, either legally because he has probable cause, or illegally. If this happens, let him search you but tell him, clearly and politely, that you do not consent to the search. The same goes for a search of your home or car.

Regardless of what happens with a cop, never resist because this will likely get you beaten and it will look bad for you in court — very likely increasing any sentence you get by *years*. If a cop begins beating you, Jim Hogshire's book *You Are Going to Prison* recommends that you lie on the ground in a fetal position and yell, "I'm not resisting."

What Police Think About Drugs

In an effort to figure out what police officers were taught about us drug users, I read several books on police psychology — that is, psychology that police use in their jobs, and not the psychology of police officers. What I found was that there really isn't much of what could be termed "police psychology." But these books do give a good indication of what cops believe about drug users.

One common belief that comes up time and again is the idea that people use drugs because they can't cope with life. Certainly this is one reason that people use drugs. But there are plenty of others: socializing, relaxation, and entertainment. But knowing that cops (and most of the rest of the world) believe the former means that you can avoid being immediately labeled a drug user (or an addict — cops don't usually think there is a difference when the drugs are illegal) if you appear confident and in control.

Another common belief is that drugs cause people to be involved with criminal activity beyond the simple fact of their illegal drug use. This is patently false regarding heroin, as I have previously mentioned. Heroin users, without other forces acting on them, are more likely to live a quiet and peaceful life than without heroin. But if you are doing something illegal, cops are going to suspect you of being a drug user. So it is best to lead the straightest life you can if you want to use heroin. And if you do something illegal, don't have drugs and paraphernalia on you at the time.

Cops also believe that drugs make users more aggressive. This is certainly true of many drugs, but not of heroin. Cops know this. The classic image of the junkie as a guy who is half awake and half asleep is a powerful one. You don't want a cop thinking you do any drugs. It isn't as though he'll overlook heroin while searching you for crack. To counter the idea that you use any drugs, be alert, clear, and calm.

Dealing with cops is never pleasant whether it is over a traffic matter or being caught smuggling a couple of kilos of heroin over the border. It is important in all such encounters to keep things in perspective. You may go to jail or you may lose your job, but you're not likely going to be killed. Keep calm and do what you can to disarm this unpleasant situation. In doing so, you may make it all go away.

The Legal System

The legal system is not in the business of dispensing justice. As far as all the people who make their livings from it are concerned, its job is to enforce laws. Certainly, there are people working in the legal system who question the laws that they help to enforce, but by and large, they are simple-minded people who think that it is wrong to break society's laws. At Nuremberg, many people were put to death for enforcing immoral laws. Unfortunately, there is no Allied Force to step in and see that justice prevails by freeing the oppressed and punishing the oppressors.

You must get out of your head any idea that you will be able to fight a charge on constitutional grounds.[4] If the Constitution meant anything, there would be no drug laws.[5] The issue is thus very clear: unless you have a lot of money to spend on your defense, if you are arrested for drug possession, you will be found guilty. The only issues up for debate are small: Of what will you be found guilty? Will you get to keep your drivers license? Will you have to spend time in jail? How long will you be on probation?

Arrest

You may think that you know the ins and outs of the legal system because you watch cop and lawyer shows. Undoubtedly, you know some things because of these shows. But the process, even when accurately portrayed, is shown from the standpoint of those other folks — the ones who get paid to be there. For you, it will be different. So let me go over the process briefly.

Under most circumstances, if a cop thinks you are guilty of a misdemeanor you will be cited. If it is a felony you will usually be arrested and taken to jail. The process of actually getting to jail can take forever. Then again, it might be quick. It really depends upon who is doing the arresting and where you are. Eventually, you will be in jail waiting for arraignment.

Own Recognizance

Once in jail, there are three possibilities. The first is that you will be "OR'ed," which is an acronym for "own recognizance,"

---

[4] Sometimes there will be reason to think that you can get off because of entrapment or an illegal search. Under most circumstances, lawyers advise against these defenses unless the case is very clear, and because the punishment for a guilty verdict is high.

[5] Perhaps you have noticed that Neo-Nazis, the KKK, and pornographers all make their way to the Supreme Court now and then. But not drug users. No one wants to touch drug users, even though they represent the most oppressed minority in this country. The ACLU is downright hostile to drug users.

which is short for "released on your own recognizance" which means they are letting you go and depending upon you to appear in court. This is the best possible situation because you get out of jail and you don't have to pay any money.

Bail

The second possibility is that you will have to post bail. Some states have set bail amounts for crimes so that you do not have to go before a judge in order to have bail set. Generally, people do not pay their bail, because it is too expensive. For example, in California the bail for possession of heroin is at least $10,000. Normally, you will contact a bail bondsman who will put up the bail for you for a mere 10% (in some states there are government issued bonds for 1%) of the total bail amount. In the California heroin case, this would be $1000. The bail bond sounds like a better idea than it is. If you happen to have the $10,000, you are better off paying it because as long as you show up to your arraignment, you will get it all back. The $1000 you paid to the bail bondsman is gone for good. And if you don't show up in court, it isn't the bondsman who is out the $10,000 — it is whoever co-signed the bond — very often you. The 10% that you pay for the bond is a stiff price for, in effect, borrowing money for a couple of days or weeks.

Jail

The third possibility is that you rot in jail until the arraignment. This is not necessarily all that bad. There are several factors to consider. How much do you dislike being deprived of your liberty? What effect will this have on your work? Is it a decent jail or is it a pit? Do you feel threatened? There is one circumstance where I think you should stay in jail: when you can blow off work, you are addicted, and the jail offers some kind of detox. In this case, jail is an opportunity (and a cheap one at that) to clean up — go for it.

Arraignment

Next comes your arraignment. If you are not in jail, make sure that you dress up for this appointment. Don't think that doing so will be seen as an obvious attempt at sucking up. There are many good reasons to dress up. First, it shows that your life is not completely out of control when you can manage to dress yourself in reasonable and clean clothes. Second, most people come to court dressed up, if you don't, you'll look bad in comparison. Third, most of the badly dressed people do a bad job (but that's still better than no job). You want to stand out to the judge as a professional — like himself — who just took a wrong turn somewhere. Further, dressing as though you have a good job reinforces in the judge's mind that you would be harmed by jail time or even very invasive drug treatment. If you don't know how to dress, check out the *Dress for Success* books — they will give you a good idea of how to dress well and, more importantly, conservatively.

When standing in front of the judge, stand tall. You aren't some street person the police just dragged in (even if you are) — try to look like the lawyers in the room. But remember that the judge is the top dog. He has so much power over you that you don't even want to think about it. Always be polite and deferential, but not obsequious. Your politeness will make up for any formal errors you may make.

People who are unfamiliar with the court system make one of two mistakes. They either talk when they should not or they let the whole procedure run over them as though they weren't even there. In court, you never speak unless you are asked to speak. Don't worry about this; you will get a chance to speak. When you get a chance to speak, do not just do as you are told — ask questions. The procedures of the court are very confusing, so make sure that you fully understand any question you are asked before you answer it. One reason for doing this is that it shows the judge that you care about what is happening and that you take the process, the court, and most importantly, him, seriously.

You have a constitutional right to a speedy trial. At your arraignment, you will be asked if you wish to waive this right. Generally, people who are stuck in jail want a speedy trial and those outside don't. But this will depend upon your schedule. This is an issue that they will often try to blow past you because by putting off your trial, it gives them more latitude in their scheduling. If you would prefer a speedy trial, say so, with all due respect. Try something like, "I'm starting a new job in a month, so I would really like to wrap this up as quickly as possible — if that works for the court."

If you have a court-appointed lawyer, you will probably not meet with him until after the arraignment. How this meeting will go will depend largely on the state in which you reside. If the state has mandatory sentencing laws, then there will be no plea-bargaining. If there are plea bargains, then the lawyer should have the offers from the prosecution. You can look at them and decide if any look palatable. In most cases they won't, but you won't have much choice but to accept them — though you may be able to counter offer for something not quite so horrible. If there is some compelling reason to believe that some procedural mistake was made while you were arrested (e.g., an illegal search), then you may discuss this. Otherwise, you will decide on a plea and discuss how best to deal with sentencing.

Punishment

Finally, you will or will not go to jail. Go into sentencing prepared to go to jail, because if you are given jail time you may be expected to go right away. Make sure that all of your business affairs are in order and all of your pressing bills paid. Find someone to manage your affairs until you get out. Your lawyer should be able to give you some idea of how long your jail time might be.

In addition to jail or in place of it, you may be given probation. There are two kinds of probation: supervised and unsupervised. For drug law offenders, supervised probation usually means that you will be drug-tested randomly and forced to go to Narcotics Anonymous meetings. Supervised probation should be avoided. In addition to the fact that it limits your life options, a single dirty urine test means you violate your probation, which can put you in jail — usually for as much as a year.

Unsupervised probation, on the other hand, is not that bad. Basically, all it means is if you are arrested again during this period, you will get harsher treatment. If you can leave the state for the term of this probation, it won't normally be a problem at all.

Parole is a legal construct that allows people to get out of jail early but without giving them complete freedom. In all particulars, it is very similar to supervised probation, though often somewhat more relaxed.

After parole or probation is over, you are free — sort of. Depending upon exactly what happened, you may not be able to vote; you may never be able to own a gun again; you may have a hard time finding a job; you will definitely be a mark for any cop who pulls you over for a burned-out tail light. What is most chilling is that if your offense was a felony, for five years afterwards you may have to register with the government as a "drug offender." Note that murderers are not required to register in such a way. Welcome to modern America!

Lawyers

Unless you can spend a lot of money on your legal defense, you are usually about as well off with a court-appointed lawyer as with anything. In most matters that come before the court, there really isn't that much that can be done about this. If there was an illegal search or cop-planted drugs on you, then you are probably better off with an attorney that you pay directly. But even then, if you don't have enough money to keep him working, he's useless.

The more complex your case is, the more a lawyer can help you. Under all circumstances, make sure that you keep in close contact with him — it's just his job, but it's your life. Make sure that he keeps you up to date on what is happening. Also be sure to get copies (and save them) of any paperwork he files on your behalf. This will keep you involved in the case, but it is also helpful to have should you switch lawyers.

Jail

Being in jail is an awful experience but by and large, it is not a life-ending one. Fear of jail often causes people to make big mistakes in managing their lives. These range from paying large amounts of money in bail to avoid a night in jail to accepting many years of supervised oppression rather than taking a much shorter stay in prison. Always remember that there are worse things than jail and, generally, two of them are supervised probation and drug treatment programs.

When you enter jail, you enter another society. This society is twisted, but it will likely seem familiar to you in many ways. In my experience, it is a lot like grammar school. The same problems you faced as a child, you will face in jail. You have to watch out for bullies; you have to get along with people from varied backgrounds — people who, with few exceptions, you wouldn't normally hang out with; you can't leave; and you get told what to do. But just as in grammar school, if you learn the ropes, you will survive.

Friends

In jail, you need as many friends as you can get. There is safety in numbers. If you get beat up in jail, it is most likely not because someone really dislikes you — though there will probably be many such people — it is because not enough people cared whether you got beat up. In addition to protecting you, friends help greatly in passing the time. Despite what you may think, the hardest thing about jail is the unrelenting boredom.

How one goes about making friends in jail is very personal. I went about it by being useful but otherwise unobtrusive. In the five months I was in, I must have written twenty-five parole petitions, a dozen sentence modifications, and countless letters. Sometimes people paid me for the work, but mostly I did it for free. As a result of this, I became sort of an institution. At times, it was a pain, with people coming to me all the time, but it gave me something to do and it protected me, because I had friends — those I had done work for and those who thought that someday I might do work for them.

Other people get by in other ways. There is a tendency, for example, for junkies to hang out with and take care of other junkies. One really obnoxious cokehead I knew got on well because he could do card tricks. Others got on well because they played basketball well or could draw. Anyone who is useful, especially in helping the time pass, will be in demand.

Regardless of how many friends you have, if you are in jail for any length of time at all, you will get into tense situations where you will say the wrong thing to someone. It is best to deal with these situations before they fester and explode. After such a situation, try to disarm it. Under most circumstances you can simply apologize, but in doing so, keep your dignity. You were wrong and you apologize. Mean it, but don't publicly flog yourself because this might well cause others to flog you too.

Scams

You must guard yourself against scams in jail. Remember where you are, after all — *some* of the inmates are in jail for real crimes. It is easiest to protect yourself if you simply "go your own way." Don't become beholden to anyone. Sadly, this advice must be applied to your fellow heroin users above all. We are not, on the whole, a very trustworthy lot. Similarly, it is a good idea to avoid betting in jail. Betting is a good way of becoming beholden to someone and even if you win, not all people are good losers.

Let me leave you with a thought about the difference between jail and prison: there isn't as much as you think. Prison is more serious than jail and your life there is likely to be much more regimented. Also, there is much more inmate-defined racial segregation in prison. Whether you are more likely to be beat up or raped in jail or prison will depend upon the prison or jail you are sent to. You are not likely to be sent to a very bad prison your first time out. Just the same, you might end up in a very bad jail.

For a thorough introduction to being in jail and prison (and also staying out) you must read Jim Hogshire's book *You Are Going To Prison*. This book leads you from the point a cop begins talking to you, all the way to frying in the electric chair. It should be read by anyone who does anything illegal (that is, everyone). However, I must caution you that the picture that Hogshire paints is more bleak than necessary. The prisons he discusses are the very worst.

Court-Mandated Treatment

Court-mandated treatment programs are a modest step towards Harm Reduction. They are the only real institutional sign that society thinks drug addiction is a medical condition and not a crime. There are variations of course, but the theme is always the same: if you go through some form of drug treatment, the state will lower the other punishment you will receive.[6] If you are lucky, this may even mean that the state will drop the charges if you complete the program. A treatment alternative is often a good idea when you are facing formal probation, because your parole officer will probably require you to participate in some form of drug "rehabilitation" anyway.

Just say, "No!"

Don't simply jump at any program that is offered. In many cases, programs are a form of double punishment, being equivalent to jail *and* a program. This may take many forms, so you must be very careful and do as much research as possible.

In the worst manifestation of this hellish form of double punishment, you are held in jail, doing "dead time" until "space opens up" in a treatment facility. This is a form of punishment that is generally meted out to those who are facing prison time. Many people are so afraid of prison that they will do anything to avoid it. I have met people who have done a year and a half in jail and then a year-long treatment program followed by a three-year joint-suspended sentence during which time they will be on formal probation. All this is to avoid a little over a year and a half in prison!

More often, the situation will look much more benign. You must do a cost-value determination: What do you get from the deal? What must you pay? Part of this last question is what you risk — this is the hardest part of the question to answer.

One thing you will *not* get is a cure for your drug addiction. There are two reasons for this. First, the level of use of most

---

[6] Note that I say "other" punishment. Treatment is punishment — just a different form.

junkies would probably not even be considered a problem if their drug of choice was alcohol instead of heroin. So even an effective treatment for drug abuse will be ineffective because the issue is not the abuse of drugs by the user — it is the abuse of the user by society.

Even if you are truly a drug addict, you will not find a cure for it in a state-mandated drug treatment program for the second reason: drug abuse treatments in widespread use are not effective.[7] Almost all such treatment programs are based upon the "12 Step" model of Alcoholics Anonymous; a system more akin to brainwashing than medical treatment. It is interesting to note that a large part of this brainwashing has to do with "going with the flow," which can only delight those already in power. "Let go, let God" is no different than "Let go, let Judge" or "District Attorney" or "Fuehrer."

If effective drug treatment is not in the deal, two things are left: less time or no time in jail and a clean (or cleaner) criminal record. For people just starting out with the legal system, these can be compelling reasons for taking a program. But there are risks and prices to pay.

The most obvious price that you will have to pay is the program itself. You will have to put up with the counseling sessions and the drug testing and whatever else is involved. Some programs require very little of the client, but others require almost complete capitulation. At the very least, this may necessitate rearranging your work schedule — which may involve telling your employer about what is going on, which may remove one of the primary reasons for going into the program in the first place.

Once you have decided that you can deal with the program itself, you must look at the odds you stand of completing it. It is critical that you find out what percentage of the clients complete the program. If most of the clients complete the program, it means that those in charge want the clients to succeed — not that the clients themselves are particularly great. On the other hand, if few complete the program (and success levels as low as 10% can be

---

[7] This is not just my opinion. This statement comes from William R. Miller and Nick Heater in their book about treatment modalities, which *are* effective, *Treating Addictive Behaviors: Processes of Change.*

found), it means that those in charge are trying to fill up the jails and prisons. Some judges weed out clients who they think may get out of the program and get re-arrested. In this way, the judges assure that they can always point to a low recidivism rate amongst their program "graduates." Any success rate below 50% should be considered unacceptable.

In addition to the overall success rate, the would-be client must look at how clients get thrown out of the program. In the harshest programs, the slightest error, such as showing up a few minutes late to a meeting, will land him in jail for a week and make him start the program over when he gets out. In such programs, clients are commonly thrown out altogether for being late too often or missing a meeting. You should not think that staying clean will be enough to get you through such a program. But not all programs are so harsh. Some programs require almost constant dirty urinalysis over a long period of time before they will give up on a client.

Regardless of how sure you are that you will make it through the program, you must look at what will happen if you fail. Failure almost always means that you will get a much harsher sentence than you would otherwise have received if you just took the punishment in the first place. Failure in a program might mean that you would have gotten off with "court" probation, but now you get a year in jail instead. This is an important consideration.

"Yes, but..."

If you decide to accept the treatment alternative, you should be prepared to take the program seriously, or at least as seriously as possible. The truth is that if you have ended up in one, you probably have gotten a little bit far out. Spending a year clean is not such a bad idea. Heroin will still be around when the program finishes. It is a good time for you to reevaluate your association with heroin.

All court-mandated treatment programs have three aspects in common: drug testing, some kind of counseling, and Narcotics Anonymous meetings (or their equivalents). If you become vested in the program in only one way, I hope it will be by staying clean while in the program. But it is possible to beat drug tests in a number of ways. Counseling can be one on one, in a group, or both. Generally, the counselor will make some kind of report to the court. As a result, you will have to do at least a little acting, even if you are vested in the program. The NA meetings are easy to deal with. In most programs you are forced to get the secretary of the meeting to sign some form, but otherwise are not required to act in any particular way.

When you first enter a diversion program, it is expected that you will be somewhat resentful and resistant. Don't feel like you have to come in with a great attitude. In fact, what the counselors are most interested in seeing is improvement. So as long as it is within reason, a bad starting attitude is a good thing.

Meetings

The clients who have been in the program longer will instruct you, by example, on how you should act. At first, you'll think that these glowing testimonies about how great their clean lives are now, are ridiculous. But over time, hopefully, you will either begin to see things that way yourself, or you will see the necessity of appearing that way. The main thing to remember about these sessions is that you are changing from your former drug-addicted self into the image your counselor sees for you.

NA meetings can be heaven or hell depending upon how you approach them. I am perhaps in the worst position of anyone I've ever met to deal with NA meetings. First, I'm an atheist and I hated all the talk about God as we understand Him. Look: this statement implies at least one thing — God is a single entity. This filters out all atheists[8] and polytheists. Furthermore, I'm an individualist and NA is a very collectivist organization. Lastly, I'm an intellectual (God help me) and NA is anti-intellectual.

But I found that I could deal with NA meetings by distracting myself. At large meetings I could read or write. At middle-sized meetings I could generally write (especially candlelight meetings). And at small meetings I could at least ask the kind of difficult NA-related questions that occurred to me: "How is it that we are pow-

---

[8] Contrary to what most people think, atheism is not the rejection of spirituality. Buddhism, for example, is an atheistic religion. An atheist is simply one who does not believe in a deity or deities.

erless over our addiction and yet we're all clean?" or, "How can NA's public relations policy be based on attraction rather than promotion when 90% of the people who come to meetings are coerced?" If you have to go to meetings, you will find a way to bear it and, who knows, maybe you'll grow to like them.

You can also cheat. The forms that the court makes you fill out are rarely scrutinized. Once you go to a single meeting, make a copy of the secretary's signature. Since secretaries don't often change, you can forge their signatures (usually this only involves tracing). Again, I don't recommend cheating; I recommend using the program and seeing if you get anything out of it. But if you want to cheat, you can — easily.

Drug Testing

I don't recommend cheating on your drug tests because the results of being caught are usually harsh — often they involve getting kicked out of the program and being sent to jail. But in many programs, it is possible to work around the drug tests.

Most programs do not test on weekends (but some do — it's just the luck of the draw). Since heroin stays in your system about 72 hours, you can use with relative safety on Friday night because it gives you at least 60 hours clean before you have to test. And even if you end up testing positive, it will only be seen as a relapse. You will probably get punished with more meetings or even a little jail time, but it won't be anything too bad.

Exactly how long heroin will be detected in your urine will depend upon how concentrated your urine is. Under no circumstances give the testing facility your first urination of the day because this is the most concentrated urine as far as drugs and other "pollutants" are concerned. Always drink a lot of water when facing a urine test — this will decrease the concentration of heroin in your urine and may give you a negative result.

You will run into drug testing in places other than diversion programs. Here I am mostly thinking of jobs that require drug testing as a pre-condition of hiring. Personally, I think that if you can't go for three days without using then you have a problem and you should skip right to Chapter Seven and start doing something about it. But if you must cheat on a drug test, there are a number of ways.

Before we start talking about ways to cheat that work, let's talk about an important way that doesn't: chemicals. Unless you know exactly what the test is being used, you cannot count on chemical additives to your urine sample. Also, don't buy those "Guaranteed Clean Drug Test" kits. They usually offer three times the purchase price if your test comes out positive. What does that matter to you if you're in jail?

If you want to check out a chemical method that works, you can do it — but it will cost you. You can buy home drug tests. These were designed by evil companies preying on other evil companies over-reacting to evil propaganda from our evil government. Tests of this sort are not the same as those that you will be subjected to in a court or employment situation, but they will show you if some chemical causes a sudden change in test results.

The classic procedure for cheating involves using a "false bladder." In this procedure, you use something along the lines of an enema bag. The person has some vessel, which holds clean urine. This false bladder is engineered in such a way so that it looks like the person is urinating, but instead he is releasing urine from the bag.

For a man, a tube runs from the bag to his penis. The bag must be placed in a location where the man can control the pressure on it. Under the arm is probably the most common location for this bag, because he can apply pressure (and thus start the urine flow) by pressing his arm against his torso. The problem with this procedure is that the apparatus is rather involved and prone to leaking. For someone mechanically inclined, however, this method may be very rewarding.

For a woman, the false bladder is placed inside the vagina itself. In this case, a plastic enema bottle is used. It will be necessary to drill a small hole in the bottom of the bottle to facilitate drainage. In addition, most women will need to keep the cap on the top of the bottle because the vaginal muscles will always apply some pressure and so the bottle will leak. If a cap is used, the woman will need to remove it to start "urinating." The false bladder procedure for cheating on urine tests is particularly effective for women. In fact, I have interviewed a number of women who have beaten urine tests using this method under the strictest of circumstances.

A related method is self-catheterization — the process of filling one's own bladder through the urethra; you can think of it as reverse urinating. This is far more practical for women than for men, but either can do it. Doing this requires paying attention to a number of details, but when done correctly, it is a perfect "cheat," it simply cannot be detected. Only people with medical training should consider trying this method.

Many testing facilities do not watch you urinate but rather test the temperature of the urine as a check for veracity. In this case, a woman may carry a vial in her vagina and a man may carry it taped next to his testicles.

Under all circumstances, the methods of conjuring will always work. As long as you can misdirect the attendant, you will have no problem. At my most recent testing facility, the procedures were quite invasive, requiring an attendant who stood outside the room watching through a window, to actually see the urine coming out of my penis. But this same place had stacks of sample cups. It was an easy matter to steal a cup, fill it with "clean" urine, and hide it. Once at the facility, one could simply switch cups in the time it took the attendant to move from the window to the door. Once home, you could clean the dirty container and use it for the following visit. For an introduction to the skills of misdirection, see Dariel Fitzkee's *The Trick Brain*.

There are two other issues regarding cheating on drug tests. The first is that you need to get some clean urine — which usually means asking one of your friends. Some people get it from their children. Regardless, I don't think it's a very nice thing to do to your friends and family. The second is that you need to have a little experience with the testing facility before you can reasonably cheat at the drug test. This either means being clean at the beginning or getting some kind of introduction to the facility. One way of doing this is to call up and ask for a tour: tell them you just got a government contract and that it requires you to drug test your employees or some other such nonsense.

Final Thoughts

Dealing with the legal system, unless you're paid to do so, is never fun. You should try your best to never enter the legal system. The best way to limit your exposure is to limit your heroin use. If you use enough for long enough, you will find yourself in jail. This is an unfortunate reality of our current laws and the laws of probability.

Chapter Six
Social Issues

No one does heroin in a vacuum. There are many relationships which will be part of your using and many that are outside of your using. It is very important to keep these relationships in order. People that are involved with drug use can harm you by their actions. They may do so directly (such as when they rip you off) or indirectly (when they lead the police to your house). Straight people can harm you, too, generally they believe it's "for your own good," but you can also harm them by causing unnecessary worry. This is why it is usually best if your straight friends and family do not learn of your heroin use.

Conversely, your social relationships also provide one of the strongest deterrents to addiction. They provide a good barometer of your heroin use. Heroin addiction usually accompanies progressive alienation from one's friends and family. Good relationships are usually a sign of a healthy person.

People in Your Neighborhood

A straight person is allowed the luxury of pretending that diversity means skin color. "We have a diverse neighborhood — why look, just across the street there's an African American man who dresses just like me, eats the same food as me, and is hysterical about illegal drugs just like me. Isn't diversity wonderful!" Unless they live in the inner city, people who don't do illegal drugs — and a lot of pot smokers, too — think that heroin is a drug used by people who are very far removed from their own world. But the fact is that about 1% of the population uses heroin (only about one in five of these are addicts), so those straight folks are fooling themselves. They probably don't have a close friend who uses heroin, but they have interactions with heroin users quite often.

What do you suppose they would do if I were to suddenly reveal all of the seemingly normal people who are actually heroin users? I think most of them would reconsider their preconceptions of what a heroin user is. Unfortunately, this will not happen. When heroin users are "outed," it is always done one at a time so that people can hang on to their preconceptions and justify their continued hatred of this group.

Humans are naturally xenophobic. That is, they mistrust that which is foreign and as a defense mechanism, they try to convince themselves that everyone they know is just a slight variation on themselves. I've often wondered what real diversity in the President's cabinet would look like. Certainly, we would get better drug leadership if a junkie were to become Drug Czar.

There are a couple of special classes of straight people that are worth noting. The first is friends and family. This group can act as a barometer of your drug involvement and this is a critical issue because no activity, drug related or not, should result in you becoming alienated from your community (defined here as the people who are close to you). Look at your friends and family this way: you don't want heroin to become a big enough part of your life so that they find out about it.

The second class is employers. Having your employer find out that you use heroin can be as bad as having the police find out. You can lose your job or, as seems to be more common these days, be forced into drug treatment. There is more to keeping your employer ignorant than not using on the job (although this is an important prerequisite). You need to use so that it does not affect your work. Even if you might have stayed up all night drinking in the past, things have changed. Now you're doing heroin and the consequences are much greater. And don't let your fellow employees know about your use either. There are any number of reasons why they might turn you in.

The point of all this is that you don't want straight people to know that you're a heroin user. Your exposure will not cause them to be more tolerant of heroin users. They will instead react the way they do when they find out that a child molester lives on their street (although generally less publicly). Their concerns will be: you'll bring a bad element to the neighborhood, you'll expose their children to heroin, you'll become violent while under the influence, you'll get desperate and steal from them, and that you're a bad and dangerous person — they just hadn't noticed it before. Any straight person who finds out that you are a heroin user will at least tell others, which increases your risk that someone will tell your employer or the police. And the really terrible thing is that they will claim to be doing it for your own good — as though losing your job or spending a year in jail is helpful.

But there is one good thing about straight people: they wouldn't know heroin if it grew on their well-groomed lawns. A straight person seeing white powder heroin will assume that it is cocaine; black tar heroin will appear to be hash. By and large, they don't know the signs of heroin intoxication; at worst they'll probably think that you're drunk. On the other hand, they know what syringes look like, so you'd better keep those well hidden. Remember, most people are afraid of heroin because of the syringe.

You should avoid contact with straight people when you are using, especially during the day. At night it is harder to see and it is more acceptable to be drunk — hell, your straight neighbor may be drunk. Even still, heroin is best shared with other heroin users. If you're throwing a barbecue for the neighborhood, don't use during it. Don't get high and then mow the lawn (there are a couple of reasons not to do that). It's perfectly all right to go out while high but do just that: go out — don't hang around with straight people you know. And take a cab or other public transportation.

Lovers

A common effect of heroin is the intense itch that people feel when they first start using the drug. This effect is the most obvious aspect of a subtle effect of heroin (so subtle in fact that it is very rarely mentioned in the scientific literature): heroin increases one's sensitivity to and the pleasure derived from the touching sensation. Heroin is a sensuous drug with the power to turn a stoic cerebral person into a grape-eating hedonist.

This aspect of heroin can make it a wonderful "couple's drug." If the dose is kept reasonably low, heroin can be very well used as a sexual aid. But you have to work at it. It is very easy for two people to use heroin together and then to just sit by themselves in their own euphoric worlds. While this can be fun, you deprive yourself of a great deal of pleasure by doing so.

Using heroin to increase intimacy between you and your partner starts with administration. Whatever method of administration you choose can be done together; however, smoking really is the best. There are two reasons. First, smoking almost requires two people in order for it to be done correctly. Second, it is the easiest method with which to control your level of intoxication. But regardless of your administration method, do it together.

After administration, consider cuddling or some other form of light petting that you enjoy. It is very nice to have your lover scratch or massage you. Of course, this is usually true even when straight. A surprising thing about heroin intoxication is that being the "doer" is at least less painful and boring — often, it in itself is quite pleasureful. This shouldn't be surprising — just sitting around on heroin is less painful and boring. This activity can often go on for many hours.

You need to remember that sex while under the influence of heroin is a process-oriented activity. Neither men nor women are likely to climax, regardless of the intensity or length of the endeavor. But by and large, this is the extent of the dysfunction; generally, men can maintain erections and women maintain acceptable levels of lubrication. This, of course, is assuming that you want to go this far — you may never get past cuddling on the couch.

One might think that when both members of a couple use heroin they are less likely to fall into addiction — two heads are better than one. This is too often not the case. Instead, good chipper behavior is like two links of a chain for couples: strain one of the links, and it's all over. Heroin couples need to pay close attention to their behavior, especially their tendency to hold conversations in which they talk each other into misbehaving.

Heroin is a very pleasurable drug, so there is always going to be a little voice inside your head that's saying, "Use it again!" Most of the time it isn't too hard to control this voice. But if you have two such voices, they can build each other up to the point where you start making bad decisions.

Often, heroin users find themselves in love with a non-user. In this case, heroin can cause a lot of strain in your relationship. This is particularly true if your partner doesn't do any drug. Unintoxicated people feel that they don't have the attention of intoxicated people — and they're right. Intoxication makes people more introverted. It puts them more inside their own heads, even if it makes them more outgoing. If you have a non-drug-using lover, you should either be straight around him or find a new lover.

On the other hand, if your lover is doing drugs — but not heroin — then it is unfair for him to object to your use of heroin. Of course, if he is drinking a couple of glasses of wine while you're passed out for hours after injecting a gram of smack, he may have something to complain about. Partners mostly get upset because you are much more inebriated than they are. This is why when a couple chooses different drugs, they face greater problems. When you are both drinking or smoking pot or whatever, you can better assess if the other is getting ahead of you or behind you. When the drug is different, it is harder. Also, you aren't doing it together, so it separates you.

If, for whatever reason, your heroin use is bothering your lover, consider not doing it around him or getting rid of him. There is no reason to let it torture either of you. If you choose to not use around your partner, you may be faced with the impulse to lie. If you want your lover to never know about your use, then never tell him. Once you've told him, trying to hide it will affect your relationship badly because you're trying to hide from him an activity of which he disapproves. As a result, he'll be wondering if you're doing it when he's not around. And you will be telling him in many subtle ways that you are doing it, which will only decrease the quality of his life and your relationship.

I will leave you with one warning: when your partner is using another drug, there will be a strong tendency to mix drugs. Remember that this is a very dangerous activity, especially when the other drugs are depressants to the central nervous system. Heroin is a relatively long-acting drug, so don't lose site of the fact that you are still using even if you aren't doing it at one-minute intervals as when you drink.

Junkies

There are a lot of social aspects to using heroin; no one does heroin alone. Even if you are a very casual user, you will most likely know at least a few other users and probably at least one addict. To begin with, you need someone to acquire the heroin from. So regardless of how much you may wish to stay away from the heroin scene, you will always be part of it — at least to a small extent. This is where the worst part of the social aspects of heroin comes in. At a minimum, you will be lied to and cheated.

Problems

I used to have an acquirer who lived in New York City. He was also a good friend. I had decided that I would vacation one year in New York and he offered his place to me while I was in town. Given the fact that he owed me $400, this gesture on his part was not all that kind. When I got into town, I found that he had decided to become clean and felt that I couldn't stay with him because it would tempt him to use again. So I ended up spending $100 a night on a hotel and he disappeared. By the end of my stay, he was using again and I was out several hundred dollars.

This is a pretty typical story of how chippers and junkies interact. In the end, he felt pretty bad about what had happened. But from my end, that didn't really matter; he was just another junkie, whether using or clean, who was incapable of seeing beyond his own immediate needs and desires. Don't ever fall into the trap of thinking that a junkie is your friend. He may be helpful in getting you drugs or something else, but remember to treat him like you would a business acquaintance: always polite, always friendly, always on guard. If he needs to borrow money, get something in return for it, such as an introduction to his connection.

It would be wrong to think that all junkies are the same, because they definitely are not. This is a point that most straight people miss — how else could the population justify sending a junkie away to prison for ten years? But you need to be careful in dealing with junkies because, by and large, they are a desperate group. A junkie's life is hard — hopefully harder than you can imagine, but try. Imagine that you have an ailment, which causes you great pain — so much pain that you cannot function. What is more, you know that there is a drug that will take away all of your pain. But you have to pay extraordinary amounts of money for it, not because the drug is expensive, but rather because society has decided that you should suffer. Such a situation might make you desperate — it might make you abandon all of society's laws — it might make you steal from your friends and family. Junkies don't live in a world *like* that — they live in *that world*.

Bad Influence

But it is not just fear of theft that should cause you to keep your distance from all junkies. To begin with, if you hang out with junkies, you will become one (see *The Making of a Junkie* on page 133) — there is really no question of this. Junkies can also increase your threat from law enforcement. Asset forfeiture is alive and well in the United States and it is not inconceivable that a law enforcement agency would let a junkie go in exchange for information on a chipper who has a lot of property to seize. But even if a junkie doesn't turn you in, police may be following him — to your house. So watch out for this. Finally, junkies will make you feel bad. There is no junkie whose life is not at least partly pathetic. All this will do is increase the pain in your life because there's nothing that you can do for a junkie. A junkie will be a junkie until he decides not to be. It is not your responsibility to keep junkies safe and warm. The fact of the matter is that most junkies get more money than you do. Their situation in life comes from their choices. So keep a healthy distance between your junkie acquaintances and yourself.

Helping

The other side of this is that once a junkie decides to get clean — and they all do — you should cut him a little slack. That doesn't mean that you have to invite him to live with you, but just being willing to talk to an ex-junkie is often a big deal because many people won't even do that much. It is natural to treat as suspect a junkie who is recently clean. But do what you can — what you feel comfortable with — for the new ex-junkie; the road away from heroin addiction is a hard one that requires a lot of gumption.

Other Drug Addicts

Then there are the other drug addicts. If you get burned trying to score on the street, most likely it will be a crack addict who burned you. As if all the pain and suffering that cops, dealers, and junkies dispense isn't enough, you have to deal with other drug addicts. Don't let any of the "addiction is a disease" propaganda fool you: all addicts are not created equal. There is a very clear distinction between those who prefer uppers and those who prefer downers.

Downer addicts are at least harmless when they are high. Upper addicts, in addition to being more outgoing and "in your face" to begin with, are pushed to new heights of obnoxiousness while under the influence. Even though alcohol is technically a downer, it acts the same way because of the peculiarities of that drug. Avoid such people: they will hurt you at worst and ruin your high at best.

Dealers

If junkies are not your friends, then dealers are just one step up from cops. I used to call one dealer every morning at 9:00 a.m. and buy $100 worth of heroin. Every morning. Did that mean that my dealer would cut me a little slack at the end of the month when things were a little lean? No way! I could get an occasional $40 front, but that was about it. Dealers would prefer that you not die, but other than that, you are nothing but an entry in their ledgers.

There is a little thing called the "thieves paradox," which is very applicable to interactions with dealers. It goes like this: you want to buy some heroin from your dealer. He's going to sell you a gram for $200. But you have to do the deal on the street, so you can't just exchange the money and drugs lest a cop sees you and throws you into jail. So instead, you exchange paper bags. In theory, yours contains $200 and his contains a gram of heroin — hopefully pretty pure at that price.

The paradox is how you and the dealer will ever manage to complete a transaction, since it is in the best interest of both to leave the bag empty. If you put the money in the bag, then there are two possible outcomes: either you get your drugs (a fair deal) or you get nothing (burned). If, on the other hand, you put nothing in the bag, then the two possible outcomes are better: either you get your drugs (free drugs) or you get nothing (a fair deal). The same paradox applies to the dealer.

There are details about your relationship which make it possible to do business and these are the details that you must keep in mind when doing business with your dealer. The first, and most important, is the fact that a real dealer wants to form a relationship with you. He wants to make thousands of dollars off you over the year instead of a couple hundred by ripping you off once. Another important detail is what I call the crowbar factor: a person ripping off junkies (on the streets, we're all junkies) will soon find a crowbar merged with his head. Another important detail is that drugs are not distributed in paper bags and so the buyer can judge, to some extent, if everything looks right.

The "thieves paradox" has been made into a computer contest. In it, various computer programs interact with one another to see which ones do the best — that is, which ones get burned the least and have successful transactions the most. Very complex programs have been developed to compete in this competition, but a consistent winner is the very simplest, a program called "Tit for Tat." We can learn much from this program.

"Tit for Tat" has a very simple two-step algorithm. If it is interacting with another program that it has not interacted with before,

"Tit for Tat" chooses to be a nice guy: put the money or the drugs in the bag. Otherwise, it does whatever you did to it last time. If you ripped it off last time, it will rip you off next time. If you honored your agreement last time, it will honor its agreement next time.

This is how you need to treat dealers. Start by trusting that they will honor their deal. But if they rip you off, rip them off back — but not if you think they'll kill you. In doing this, you let them know that you're a good customer but you aren't going to allow them to abuse you. This information may find its way to other, more ethical, dealers too. And this can only improve your entire drug buying experience.

This brings up an important issue: it is better to have more than one dealer. When I first had multiple dealers, I felt kind of guilty about it, like I was being unfaithful. So I hid this fact as best I could. But I later learned that doing just the opposite was better. If a dealer thinks he is the only one or that he is the most convenient one, he will abuse you. He will never give you any deals, he will make you wait longer, and he will refuse to come by at any but his "regular" hours. By having more than one dealer, you can abuse them all to your advantage. Are your dealers taking too long to come by? Page them all, buy from the first one, and tell the others that you got tired of waiting. They'll be pissed off, but so what? What are they going to do? Turn you in to the police? Refuse to make gobs of money by selling to you? Forget about it.

Another way to abuse your dealer is to tell him that you are doing poor financially. If he wants $100 for 6 bags, tell him you only have $90. Be sure to lay it on thick. It doesn't even matter if your dealer doesn't speak English — he'll get the idea. If your dealer ever gets the idea that you have a lot of money, he will abuse you and feel good about it. Remember that he is making at least a 100% profit (although it can be as much as 500%). He's not going to walk away from a deal because of a few dollars, especially if he knows you can just call someone else.

Don't ever fall into the trap of worrying what your dealer thinks of you. You have a business relationship with him and that relationship will continue as long as you have money and want to do business with this dealer. He may think that you're a pain but that will only help you. The squeaky wheel may get the grease, but it also gets the best deals and service. If you start thinking that your dealer's thoughts and feelings matter, you will allow him to abuse you.

The Making of a Junkie

There is little in the considerable scientific work on addiction that is actually helpful. But the work of Dr. Norman Earl Zinberg at Harvard is a wonderful and notable exception. One reason that he was able to revolutionize the science of addiction was that he did not focus his attention on addicts, as most researchers do. He studied many responsible users — most notably, heroin chippers. What he discovered is still highly controversial:[1] usage of a drug will be largely controlled by the community in which the drug is ingested.

What this means specifically is that if you use around chippers, you are likely to stay a chipper and if you use around junkies you are likely to become a junkie. The process of becoming a junkie happens internally long before it happens in fact. The user will begin by redefining "junkie" in his head. This process will be very slow, but it will cause "junkie" to stop being a pejorative. Eventually, "junkie" will have positive connotations for him. He will begin to see himself more and more in the role of a junkie. It will become comfortable. And then he will be a junkie.

Because of this process, you should limit your interactions with junkies. When dealing with chippers, there will be built-in social structures that will protect you from addiction. Friday night you might use heroin, but Saturday night everyone is going out danc-

---

[1] The addiction treatment community is under the intellectual dictatorship of the "addiction as disease" philosophy. Although this theory has been repudiated scientifically, it still keeps a tight grip on treatment, especially in the United States. Discoveries such as Dr. Zinberg's are seen as an attack on the establishment because they imply that addiction is a behavioral problem, which can be fixed, rather than a physical problem, that is chronic.

ing. So you go out dancing instead of using. But the junkies are using Friday night, and Saturday morning, and Saturday night. If you're with them, most likely you will be using too.

But just because you're in a group that uses responsibly is no guarantee that *you* will use responsibly, just as hanging out with junkies is no guarantee that you will use irresponsibly. All this socialization does is improve your odds. In the end, using responsibly is up to you.

The main theme of Zinberg's work is: chippers have rituals they follow, which keep them from becoming junkies. The whole point of this book is to provide you with those rituals. They include: staying as far out of the junkie subculture as possible, clean administration, and limited usage frequency. These rituals keep chippers from becoming junkies.

Old Junkie Tales

There are a lot of stories that one hears as a heroin user that run anywhere from true to absolutely false, from harmless to deadly. In this section I list a few of these stories in order to explain and correct what heroin users tell themselves. I call them "Old Junkie Tales" because they are passed down from generation to generation without much thought given to their validity. They are part of heroin culture.

Heroin is more euphoric than morphine. This story goes that heroin is primarily morphine, but that it has something extra that makes you real happy. This mistaken belief is undoubtedly based upon a couple of things. First, it's pretty hard to get your hands on morphine, so most users have never actually tried it. The second is the fact that heroin is more potent than morphine — three times as potent. When heroin and morphine are given intramuscularly to addicts, they notice no difference. A small difference is noted when the drugs are taken intravenously.

Heroin has a greater rush than morphine. This is not an "old junkie tale," but rather an "old doctor tale." Robert L. Dupont, MD, in his generally terrible book *The Selfish Brain: Learning* *from Addiction* (with an inspiring foreword by that noted addiction scientist Betty Ford), states that there is no need to have heroin in the pharmacopoeia because its only advantage is that it has a greater rush associated with it. He bases this statement on the fact that heroin crosses the blood-brain barrier faster than morphine. This is completely wrong, and a modest understanding of statistics proves it. (But since when have Drug Warriors ever been concerned with facts?) Heroin is actually a better drug to be used for pain management than morphine. First, it does not have the problem of the lethal histamine release of morphine. Second, for patients needing high doses of either pain reliever, heroin is more soluble and thus may be administered in larger quantities.

Dilaudid is not as euphoric as heroin. It is commonly believed that while hydromorphone is much stronger than heroin, it is not as euphoric. This is not true. In fact, hydromorphone is less nausea-producing and so may well be more euphoric.

You can't get addicted if you don't inject. Addiction to heroin has nothing whatsoever to do with the administration route. Addiction develops based upon frequency of use only. The amount used will determine how dependent upon heroin the user becomes, however. Thus, addicts who do not mainline the drug will generally have more mild withdrawal symptoms. But even this is not always the case.

Milk mixed with heroin reduces the possibility of overdose. This is a curious tale. Not only is it not true, mixing heroin with milk and injecting it is more likely to cause medical problems and sudden death than injecting heroin alone. This tale probably comes from the fact that white powder heroin is often cut with milk sugar; a sample of heroin with a lot of milk sugar in it is probably less likely to cause an overdose because it has so little heroin.

Heroin mixed with alcohol can kill you. Junkies used to tell each other this in the 1940s but for some reason they stopped — the result being that many junkies now die each year because they combine heroin and alcohol. This is a story that junkies and chippers need to start telling each other again. It is the single most important thing to know about using heroin.

It only takes a week to detox from heroin. After a week, you are detoxed to the extent that there is no more heroin in your body, but you'll still feel pretty crummy for a good month or two. The main problems are depression and insomnia. Many addicts relapse after the first week because they still feel bad even though everyone has told them that they should be feeling fine. They figure that the only way they will ever feel better is by using. They do, in fact, have another option: wait another week or two.

It takes years for your brain chemistry to return to normal after heroin addiction. It can take three to six months for your brain chemistry to return to normal, but most people feel pretty normal after about a month. Antidepressants can be invaluable in shortening this period of time.

Addiction is a disease. Addiction is not a disease. Physical dependency is a condition but not a disease. Addiction itself is a behavioral dysfunction that under most circumstances can be treated the same way as any self-destructive behavior. If you are addicted to heroin, it does not even mean that you are prone to addiction. Heroin is a very addictive substance. Anyone who does heroin often enough will become addicted to it. Literally millions of people have gotten over heroin addiction.

You can become addicted to heroin after trying it once. In terms of physical addiction, this is patently false. Some people do, however, run head-long toward addiction after their first use because they love it so much. But such a person is very rare indeed. And even such a person, if he could not acquire heroin, would experience no withdrawal symptoms.

It takes a month of daily use to become addicted to heroin. The truth is that the time it takes to become physically addicted to heroin varies from person to person. Addiction is not a binary process: for example, at 5:03 a.m. I am not addicted, but at 5:04 a.m. I am. Most people feel distinct withdrawal symptoms after five days. Even after three consecutive days of use, most people have trouble sleeping. So it can't be said exactly how long any given person will take to become addicted. What can be said is that using every day for a week will certainly result in you experiencing some withdrawal symptoms.

Once you become addicted to heroin it is easier to become readdicted. This is possibly true, but I haven't found any scientific evidence that supports it. In addition, my own experience contradicts this notion. This idea seems to stem from the fact that once a person has experienced withdrawal, he knows what symptoms to watch out for. As a result, he can become hypersensitive to any ache and pain that he feels and blame it on heroin addiction. Repeated studies have shown that 30% of the people who go to methadone clinics for detox are not, in fact, physically addicted to heroin. Don't become a heroin hypochondriac.

Dealers give away drugs for free to get you hooked. This is the idea that suppliers of illegal drugs are "pushers" — people luring customers into their web of life-long drug addiction. In fact, there is plenty of demand for drugs — dealers do not need to create any more.

Heroin is cut with strychnine. What drug dealer would kill his cash cow? This myth does have a basis in fact, however. Heroin is sometimes cut with strychnine for users who wish to smoke it. Cutting heroin with strychnine lowers the melting point of the combination and thus provides a greater rush. Regardless of the administration route, any strychnine in a bag of heroin will almost certainly be too little to harm the user.

The Social Drug

Many drugs are considered social. Heroin is not. This is unfortunate and even dangerous. The drugs that are considered social are also the ones that are most likely to make people angry and violent. Heroin makes its users more tolerant of others and in this sense, is an excellent social drug. When taken in moderate doses, heroin can be an excellent enhancement to social interactions.

Social interactions are where we see most clearly the distinction between heroin being part of your life and being your life. If heroin makes your social interactions more pleasant, then it is a good addition to your life. But if it pushes people away and causes you to become alienated from other human beings, then it is a bad thing.

The worst part of allowing your social life to slip away is that it removes an important safety mechanism, which prevents heroin addiction. You need to keep your straight friends. But just as important is that you need to make sure that your user friends are responsible about their use. Doing so increases your safety and quality of life in innumerable ways.

Chapter Seven
Addiction

Even with the best of intentions, people get addicted to heroin. It is easy to do, and after becoming addicted, fear of withdrawal symptoms often leads to a worse addiction. It doesn't matter why or how you got yourself addicted. Being addicted to heroin is a simple fact and it does not say anything about where you've been and it doesn't say anything about where you'll go.

A big reason that people fear heroin is that it is a very addictive drug. This is funny, given that while most people can define what addiction is, they cannot tell you what would make one drug more addictive than another. Heroin is highly addictive in that it does not take all that long to become physically dependent upon it, and withdrawing from heroin is pretty nasty. But what truly makes one drug more addictive than another is how dependent upon the drug your body gets. In this case, heroin is not that addictive. Remember this: if you stop using heroin, it will not kill you. Long time alcohol addicts must get medical attention when they stop using; heroin users can go it alone.

If you're okay with your addiction, that's great. Some people can keep their lives together and stay addicted. As I've noted before, we are a country of caffeine addicts, so there is nothing particularly bad about being an addict in and of itself. If you've read this book up to this point, you know most of the consequences of your actions.

A lot of people avoid dealing with their addictions because they think that they will have to give up all drugs, turn Christian, and walk around quoting from *It Works: How and Why.* This is not the case. In fact, there are many addicts who have gotten clean and gone on to be chippers. Of course, this is not the case for all addicts.

How well you will "recover" from your addiction depends upon who you are. I've been to many Narcotics Anonymous meetings where every person in the room who talked demonstrated that he was as screwed up *off* drugs as he was *on* them. You need to ask yourself some questions about your life before you became a heroin user: were you able to make ends meet? take care of your family? did you have emotional problems? anger? depression? These are not easy questions to answer because every person on the planet could answer "yes" to each and every one of them. Everyone gets down now and then. This is not the same as chronic depression. A good indication that you are chronically depressed is that you've tried to kill yourself or that you've thought about it a lot (apart from your addiction). The overall question is: Was your life together before heroin? Chances are that if it wasn't before, it won't be afterwards.

There are addictive personalities and addictive drugs. Heroin is an addictive drug and anyone who uses long enough with sufficient frequency will become addicted. No one is immune. If you have succumbed to the powers of heroin for the same reason, you stand a very good chance of leaving heroin behind completely, or regaining your chipper status.

The most common reason addicts give for staying on heroin is that it will be painful to get off. While this is true to some extent, it does not have to be all that painful. The detox experience can run anywhere from "barely noticeable" to "where's my shotgun? I'm going to kill myself." And the worst detox is not necessarily unmedicated cold turkey. I paid almost $10,000 for my worst detox. Detox from heroin can be relatively painless and cheap and, in the end, safe.

Why Heroin Addiction Sucks

Most people couldn't tell you why addiction sucks. I can't do it in general terms, but I can with specifics. Heroin addiction gets in the way of living your life. This is why I brush off psychological addiction. If, after a hard work week, you get hammered on smack during your days off, how does this hurt you? Even if you really need to use on the weekend, how does it get in the way of living your life? Sure, you might be able to come up with some superfluous reasons, but there is nothing soft about the ways that physical addiction adversely affects your life.

Let me take you on a little journey into my world of heroin addiction. At my worst, I was using $200 of very good quality heroin per day. As a result of my large habit, I needed to use roughly every six hours. This represents a fairly extreme case. I've known addicts who used more heroin than this, but most use substantially less. Most addicts don't start to feel bad for at least 12 hours after using and, even for them, things do not get really bad until about 24 hours. So the problems I'll discuss will likely be worse than they are for most addicts, but they will all be experienced by all addicts — just to lesser degrees.

I couldn't sleep without shooting up. If I was low on money, I would be awake until I found enough for a fix. This, and the fact that I knew that it would not be long before I started to have uncontrollable diarrhea and vomiting often left me in a state of near panic. I would try to plan ahead, but this wasn't always possible. During these periods, I did my most shameful things — things that even today I shudder to think about.

There was never a feeling of waking up fresh, energetic, and happy. Instead, I woke up sweating, with chills, and often nausea. Just as caffeine addicts groggily drag themselves to their coffee makers in the morning, I had to "brew" my heroin, get it in a syringe, and then inject it into a vein. Unlike a coffee addict who can just drink his drug, I was forced to inject my drug — a procedure that takes a great deal of skill and dexterity — when I was not in top form.

I've heard coffee addicts complain that they have to make sure that they have coffee in the house before they go to bed. Otherwise, they will have to get up in the morning and go and buy it. "What lucky addicts!" I always thought. Heroin dealers can be hard to find at 7:00 a.m. There were mornings when I waited, vomiting into a bowl, hours for my dealer to show up.

Travel has never been one of my great loves. I'm kind of a homebody. I like puttering around the house, sending out for Chinese food, and cuddling on the couch watching old movies. But when I was a junkie, I learned all about traveling, because I had to make all kinds of preparations for even the smallest excursion. A three day trip to the beach? That took at least $600 in heroin, but probably more because I was "on holiday" and wanted to relax. Plus, I would need at least 20 syringes and all of my paraphernalia. Then I had to hide all of this stuff very carefully in the car so I didn't have to worry about a police search.

International travel is basically out unless you know that you can quickly get a connection in the country you're traveling to. And even then, you need enough to get you there. In my case, this was a fair amount. Given all of the drug trafficking laws, you can count on being searched and maybe even being strip-searched. You also have to worry about the drug laws of the country you're going to.

Once you have a habit as big as mine, you are never well for more than a few minutes. It's like you're a little sick all of the time. I had a constant runny nose, my muscles ached, and I just felt crummy.

There are a million little things that you notice while addicted. One is that I had to dress for my habit — I always wore long-sleeved shirts. I had to learn to apply makeup to cover up the track marks on my hands. I had to shoot up before any kind of intense work like a job interview or a lecture. Taking care of these "little things" occupied a large fraction of my time.

By far, the worst thing about being a junkie was that I did all of this work just to stay well. I very rarely got high and when I did, it only lasted a few minutes. In retrospect, I don't know why I stayed addicted for such a long time. Chipping was fun; addiction sucked.

Warning Signs

For a lot of drugs, it can be pretty easy to say, "I'm not addicted." But for heroin, there really isn't a lot of doubt. Heroin lets you know. If you suffer from withdrawal symptoms when you don't use for a while, then you are addicted.

Some people claim to be addicted when they only use every other day. This is highly unlikely unless the addict has a low tolerance to withdrawal symptoms — and this may be the case. More likely, such a person is not addicted, but soon will be. This is a sad behavior that I have seen in many users. A chipper will begin to push the envelope of safe usage by using more and more frequently. He won't be addicted, but he will think that he is. His belief in his addiction will cause him to use even more frequently until he reaches the point that he is indeed addicted.

You can check to see if you are addicted very easily. Just stop using. After 24 hours, you should begin to feel some of the withdrawal symptoms. Generally, these will be minor: crawling skin and sweating. Sometimes you will feel sicker. You may experience vomiting and diarrhea. It is highly dependent upon your body and how accustomed it is to heroin. One thing that should encourage you to get clean as soon as possible is that the shorter your run (regardless of the amount you used), the shorter and less painful your detox will be.

Some of the warning signs include:

Increased Consumption: Before you become addicted, there are warning signs that your use is getting out of hand. The biggest sign is that your consumption or frequency of use is increasing. This is not a good sign, regardless. For one thing, this can cost you a fortune. The rules for staying unaddicted are clearly delineated in Chapter Four. If you are getting anywhere near the borders of these guidelines, then you should take a look at your usage.

Obsession: Obsessing is a *bad* sign. As I've stated before, heroin is part of a chipper's life. If heroin has begun to dominate your thinking, if it is the main source of joy in your life, you need to look out. Obsession can show up in other ways, such as romanticizing famous junkies. Of course, this isn't always the case. A lot of people who have never even tried heroin romanticize junkies.

Work Deterioration: Work deterioration, tardiness, and absences are all warning signs that your drug use is getting out of hand. Generally, the problem will not be that you are nodding off on the job. Most junkies still manage to do relatively little smack while at work. But staying up late using on work nights and similar behaviors can have a deleterious effect on your work. This usually indicates that you are using too much.

Greed: There is a process of drug use whereby new users are given drugs, more advanced users give away drugs to their friends, and experienced drug users hoard their drugs away and never share. This, in itself, does not indicate a problem. But if you are hoarding your drugs, you may want to take a look at this behavior and question it.

Care: You should always be very cautious with your drug use. Heroin is highly addictive. So if you are blowing off the "Rules" and making up your own, you're probably headed for a fall. The same thing goes for the care you take in your administration hygiene.

Isolation: Heroin can cause you to isolate yourself. You should watch out for the deterioration of your relationships. In most cases, this does not take the form of abusing your loved ones (leave that to the alcohol addicts). Rather, it is usually the case that you simply neglect them — rarely taking the time to call or visit. In my opinion, relationships with other people are the greatest joy in life. If you are blowing off your relationships for a drug, you've at least got your priorities out of whack and are likely addicted.

Money: Financial problems can be an indication that your use is out of control. This is why it is a good idea to keep records of your drug expenditures (but under no circumstances label them as such — you don't want to spend a year in prison just because you're a conscientious user). If you are spending 50% of your expendable income on dope, then you really need to be concerned. Similarly, you need to make sure that you aren't spending more and more money on dope each month. After a short period of time, your expenditures should stabilize. They might go up from time to time, but just the same, they ought to go down from time to time. If you're running out of money, drugs should be one of the first things to go.

Sex: As stated in Chapter Six, heroin can be a great addition to you sex life, but excessive use will have just the opposite effect. If you notice that you're getting high as a substitute for sex, then you need to cut back or even stop using.

Test Yourself

The book *How to Get Off Drugs* gives a questionnaire to determine how involved you are with heroin. Most of the questionnaire is silly, implicitly stating, "You cannot use opioids, particularly heroin, responsibly." The test indicates that the route of administration alone can determine whether you have profound involvement with the drug. I have developed my own questionnaire that is more appropriate and less biased. It is listed in Table 7.

Table 7: Opioid addiction test.

Number	Question
1.	Do you use opioids daily?
2.	Do you use opioids at least three times a week?
3.	Has there been any significant increase in your use of opioids during the past three months?
4.	Have you ever tried to quit and failed?

A "Yes" answer to any question indicates profound drug involvement if not outright addiction.

If you are using heroin every day, then you are addicted. There is no denying this. If you answer Yes to this question then you need to decide what, if anything, you are going to do about your addiction. But you cannot sit around and claim that you aren't addicted — there is no denying this.

Using opioids three times a week means one thing for sure: you are breaking the rules discussed in Chapter Four. It also means that you are either physically addicted or, much more likely, close. If you cut back now, you will save yourself a great deal of pain.

As stated previously, increased frequency and amount of use is always a danger sign. It usually does not imply that you are partying more, rather it implies that your tolerance is going up. This is one of the best reasons for not being addicted: if you continue in this path, you will never be able to get enough heroin to get high. Stay a chipper and remain able to get high.

If you have tried to stop using before and found that you couldn't, you're most likely physically addicted and have been for some time. But sometimes, chippers try to stop using and find that they can't. This isn't physical addiction and it doesn't even mean they will become physically addicted. Nevertheless it isn't a good sign. If you've found that you can't even go on a two-week vacation without using, then this is a very bad sign indeed. It probably indicates that you need to make a complete break with heroin.

All of this discussion should be of help to you in evaluating your heroin use. But the truth is, you probably already know if you have a problem or if you're headed toward one. I've already provided you with my blessings to stay an addict. If that's what you want to do, I'm sure you already know a lot of junkies who can help you to be a success in this endeavor. But if you want to get off heroin (or even just back away a little), the rest of this chapter can help.

An Overview of Detox Methods

There are a number of detox procedures and then there are a number of ways to go about these procedures. I'm not a good proponent for having some institution or professional detox you. Under these circumstances, you become just a cog in the detox machinery. They wake you up, they give you pills, they force you to go to meetings and counseling sessions, and they put you to sleep. People in these situations often lose sight of the fact that the whole process of getting off and staying off heroin is their own. Doing it yourself not only avoids this artificial process, but it also gives you a sense of accomplishment that you are less likely to throw away by going out and getting strung out again.

There are four primary treatments: opioid substitution, non-opioid medication, rapid detox, and cold turkey. Other than rapid detox, it is possible to use all of these methods in detoxing yourself. The only institution that commonly provides cold turkey withdrawal is jail and most of those offer at least some kind of medication.

Not everyone can detox themselves, however. In the next section, I will discuss what is necessary to successfully detox yourself. Even if it is possible, it may not be the best thing for you. Detox programs provide a number of benefits. First, good programs know what they are doing and they will keep you fairly comfortable and as healthy as possible. Second, they usually provide some kind of counseling after the worst of the detox is over, and this can be helpful. Third, you don't have to worry about anything.

Opioid Substitution

The idea behind opioid substitution is that pretty much any opioid will block withdrawal symptoms. If the substitute opioid is used for five days and then stopped, you will not have become dependent upon it and you will no longer be dependent upon heroin. If this sounds great, it is. There is no easier way to detox yourself. The main drawback is that you may keep using the substitute and get addicted to it. Another problem is that the horror of detox can be a powerful incentive to keep you clean. Conversely, the fact that this kind of detox is so painless may make you more likely to relapse.

The most common opioid substitute is methadone, but just about any opioid will do if you can match the dosage. It may take way too much codeine, for example, to detox even a fairly minor heroin habit. A procedure similar to opioid substitution is heroin weaning. In this procedure, you slowly cut back your usage until you can stop cold turkey. This is a lot harder than it sounds because of the variable quality of heroin, but this problem may be circumvented.

Medicated Detox

Most of the withdrawal symptoms come from a hyperactive locus coeruleus. This area of the brain contains the neuronal cells, which create norepinephrine. The primary function of norepinephrine is to help the body maintain a constant blood pressure. It does this by causing certain blood vessels to constrict and so raise the blood pressure. But it also seems to act as a brain alarm modulator, which is essential to controlling human emotions. Heroin depresses the locus coeruleus, which causes the secretion of norepinephrine to decrease. When addiction takes place, the locus coeruleus works harder at producing the norepinephrine. When the heroin is taken away, the locus coeruleus overproduces norepinephrine.

Non-opioid medication usually involves the use of Clonidine because it also depresses the locus coeruleus. Clonidine works the same way that opioid substitution does, but with the added benefit that you don't have to worry about getting addicted to something else.

In general, Clonidine is used with other drugs. Generally, benzodiazepines are given for sleep (though Clonidine helps here too), acetaminophen is given for body aches, and other medications are given for abdominal cramps, diarrhea, and depression. This kind of treatment usually involves taking a lot of pills.

Rapid Detox

There are two kinds of rapid detox. In one, you are anesthetized and your body is flooded with an opioid antagonist, which is basically a drug that competes for the body's opiate receptor sites and blocks opioids from stimulating these sites. This stuff literally rips the heroin (morphine, actually) out of your body. You go through intense withdrawal over the course of about four hours, and then you're fine. At least that's the theory. In practice, you can be very sick for many days. This sickness can be every bit as bad as cold turkey withdrawal. This method of rapid detox works best for addicts with small habits; the worse your addiction, the sicker you will be after the procedure. This procedure is also quite expensive (usually about $5000) and practically no insurance company will pay for it.

The second method of rapid detox is found in a lot of HMO plans. In it, a non-opioid treatment is combined with gradually increased doses of an opioid antagonist. The idea here is to hurry the detox process along. And it works. Generally, a person will come out of detox after three days (instead of the usual five to seven) feeling as good as they would after about two weeks. The downside is that it is pretty unpleasant. You will be given more medication than you would if you weren't being given the opioid antagonist, but it usually it isn't enough to make you all that comfortable. The plus side is that you can get in and out of treatment quickly so you can keep your old life (if you still have one).

Under no circumstances would I recommend anyone go through the full-blown rapid detox. It is only really helpful for those with minor addictions — precisely the people who would have a relatively easy time with any other treatment. In addition to its inefficacy, it is an extremely expensive procedure, which you will almost certainly have to pay for out of your own pocket.

The partial rapid detox is not such a bad idea. It will be unpleasant, but it will also help you through what I consider to be the hardest part of getting off heroin: the first two weeks after detox. It is during this time that the temptation to use is greatest because you're detoxed (at least everyone tells you that you are), and yet you feel like crap. This method will have you leaving the hospital or treatment center feeling a lot better.

Cold Turkey

Cold turkey withdrawal means that you just sit somewhere and let the illness run its course. The best thing about this is that it doesn't cost you anything. The worst thing is that if you can use, you will. It is not pleasant to live through, especially if you have a large habit. The worst aspect of the illness is that you will get almost no sleep for three full days. People are fond of saying that heroin withdrawal is nothing more than a bad flu. This is not true — it is a bad flu combined with tenacious insomnia and a clinical level of depression. A lot of the underestimation of the effects of heroin withdrawal comes from the early 1970s when the heroin was so poor that few people could afford much of a heroin habit. Times have changed; withdrawal is unpleasant.

Opioid Substitution

Methadone is the drug of choice for opioid substitution. It is used for two primary reasons. First, it is long acting so it only has to be administered once a day. The lifetime of methadone in the body is about ten times that of morphine. As a result, it takes longer to detox off of methadone — although the withdrawal symptoms are not as bad. Second, it is roughly half as potent taken orally as it is injected (as compared to heroin which is one-tenth), so it is easily administered. These reasons make methadone maintenance and detox programs relatively easy to administer.

The government does not monitor methadone clinics very well. Some of them are not well run and act as nothing more than facilities to allow addicts of one drug to become addicts of another drug. At such facilities, it is common for clients to have heroin habits on top of their methadone habits.

But methadone can be very helpful in detoxification. I once used an illegal supply of methadone to detox myself over the course of five days. I have never had such an easy detox. On the sixth day, I was able to sleep without chemical assistance, and this is quite remarkable (I was only detoxing from about $40 a day at that time, however).

Methadone by Program

Some states allow people to go through a methadone detox on an outpatient basis — others require residence. If an outpatient program is available to you, it is worth considering. There are a few issues that you should keep in mind, however.

First, try to find a short program. Twenty-one day detoxes are common. This is a good amount of time even though it does get the patient addicted to methadone. As a result of this, the last week and a half of the detox is to wean the patient off methadone. However, this is much better than detoxes of six months (or more!) duration. If you can't find a detox with a duration of less than one month, you may want to go it on your own.

Because you must be weaned from the methadone, the program you choose should provide you with some drugs to help you through the end of the detox and for the week or so afterwards. It is common to provide Clonidine as well as something to help with sleep. Unfortunately, because of the prevailing belief that if a person is addicted to one drug he is prone to addiction to all drugs, inappropriate drugs are often prescribed for sleep. In particular, large doses of tricyclic antidepressants are often prescribed instead of benzodiazepines. The benzos are really very good, with few side effects, and they are pleasant. The antidepressants have many bad side effects and will leave you groggy the whole next day. You are better off with nothing than with the tricyclics. Be sure to check out any drugs the program is offering.

Most methadone programs still get most of their money from maintaining patients rather than detoxing them. As a result, patients are usually encouraged to get on methadone maintenance. Although I truly believe that such advice is based upon an earnest belief on the part of the clinic professionals that such maintenance is a Good Thing, I equally believe that this advice is bad. Fight it. Although detoxing from methadone is not nearly as intense as it is from heroin, it is a lot longer. So limit your methadone use.

Methadone by Yourself

In order to detox yourself, you need to get enough methadone for the entire process. There are two reasons for this. First, you don't want to have to go out and get more later — for one thing, you may not be able to find any. Second, illegal methadone usually comes as a liquid and it is often cut with water. You do not want your methadone intake to oscillate up and down over the course of your detox. You want a constant concentration, whatever that may be.

Acquiring methadone is not that hard. You may be lucky enough to have a friend with chronic pain who has methadone prescribed. Mostly though, you'll be forced to find someone on a methadone program. You may be able to do this through your junkie acquaintances. Often, people will know of someone who sells methadone. If this isn't the case, look in the yellow pages and find out where the methadone clinics are in your area. Drop by in the mornings and see if you can strike up any conversations. People in such programs are often given small amounts to take home for weekends and for short trips. Sometimes, they are willing to sell part of their stash.

Be careful when scoring methadone from addicts. There is a lot of colored water sold as methadone.

Once you have acquired the methadone, divide it into five doses. You can do this in one of two ways: equal doses or decreasing doses. Equal doses are easiest to prepare, but decreasing doses have advantages. The worst of the detox takes place during the first two to three days. Having a larger dose of methadone during these days may make you more comfortable. By lowering your dose as you move through the detox, you make it easier to eventually stop. And finally, you make becoming addicted to methadone almost impossible even if you use it over a longer period of time. I suggest that you break your methadone into the following percentages: 30% (day one), 30% (day two), 20% (day three), 10% (day four), 10% (day five).

Methadone is not the only drug that you can use to detox yourself. In particular, large doses of Loperamide (Imodium), which can be purchased over the counter, can also be used. It is a mistake to use most pill opioids because they are combined with large doses of acetaminophen, which is toxic to the liver. Sometimes you can get opioids alone, such as Oxycodone as Roxicodone™, but this is mostly the exception.

You can also wean yourself off heroin using decreasing doses of heroin, but in order to do this you must stockpile a large amount before you start. I recommend weaning yourself off over the course of ten days, which is a good compromise between speed and the pain of detox. You will need about five times your daily consumption of heroin. You must then combine all of the heroin together and create ten doses: 15% (day one), 15% (two), 15% (three), 15% (four), 10% (five), 10% (six), 5% (seven), 5% (eight), 5% (nine), 5% (ten). Depending upon your usage pattern, you may wish to further divide these daily doses so that you can use twice a day.

At the end of this weaning period, you may find that you still suffer from some withdrawal symptoms. If you can get your hands on some Valium to help you sleep for a couple of days, do that.

(But don't become a Valium addict!) Imodium is quite effective for diarrhea. Marijuana is good for nausea. But, by this time, your symptoms should be relatively minor.

You must be careful when withdrawing yourself with the use of opioids. After you stop using the opioid substitute, you are not necessarily detoxed. You should not think that now you can use "just once," since you haven't used in a week. This may cause withdrawal symptoms to return. If you must use, you need to wait another week before doing so.

Medicated Detox

Modern medicine is often attacked for treating the symptoms of a disease instead of treating the disease itself. Many think that the body should be treated as a system instead of a collection of parts. There is much to be said for this criticism. However, there are many cases where treating the symptoms is the right thing to do. A good example of this is dysentery, which used to kill people (it still does in some places). It turns out that the body will cure itself of dysentery as long as it doesn't die before doing so. The main symptom of dysentery is diarrhea, so the patient needs to be treated with either something to stop the diarrhea or lots of water so that the patient does not get dehydrated — dehydration is what kills dysentery sufferers.

Withdrawal is an even stronger candidate for treating the symptoms. The disease will go away in a few days — all you want is to get through this period with as little discomfort as possible. There are pills that will take care of most of the symptoms, but you will get only the drugs that will take care of the worst symptoms, because of practical concerns such as drug interactions and cost.

This kind of treatment is often referred to as "Clonidine treatment" because Clonidine is the most important drug that you will take. If you can get nothing else, Clonidine will be enough to make even the worst detox bearable. Most of the withdrawal symptoms stem from the fact that your locus coeruleus, after being depressed because of the heroin you have been bombarding it with, becomes hyperactive. Clonidine also depresses the locus coeruleus and thus greatly reduces many withdrawal symptoms including: diarrhea, nausea, vomiting, and temperature regulation problems.

You must be careful using Clonidine, however, because it does reduce blood pressure. Because of this, some doctors are concerned about allowing addicts to use it on their own. But this is unacceptably cautious. Clonidine can cause death if given to a patient with extremely low blood pressure. Generally, it is only unsafe when the patient's blood pressure is 60 over 40 or less, and this is unlikely, especially since the lack of heroin causes high blood pressure. But because of the possible problems, you should be careful with Clonidine. Clonidine is usually distributed as Clonidine HCl in 0.1 mg tablets or patches. You should not take more than two tablets (0.2 mg) in any four-hour period — in fact, far less is usually sufficient. If your prescription indicates that you should take less, follow those instructions. Talk to your doctor if you have questions.

Try to get a little exercise before you take your Clonidine. All of the laying around that you do during detox will tend to lower your blood pressure and thus increases your risk. Just the same, be careful when moving around soon after you take the Clonidine. It can make you quite light-headed and may even cause you to pass out.

Although Clonidine will help you sleep, it will likely not be enough. The more you can sleep through your detox, the better off you will be. One reason why many people fail to complete a detox is that they get bored. Sleeping definitely makes the time pass. Some kind of benzodiazepine is usually prescribed for sleep. Benzodiazepines are roughly divided into two groups: short and long-acting. The long-acting drugs are Librium and Valium, with halflives of about two days. The short-acting drugs are Restoril (temazepam) and Xanax, with halflives of about a half-day. You are best staying with a short-acting drug because you can better control the concentration in your body. Temazepam is the best choice. If you cannot get a prescription, you can use alcohol. I recommend against using alcohol, however, as it has many disadvantages. Benzodiazepines affect the brain very similarly to alcohol but alcohol will increase the intestinal problems associated with your withdrawal. Also, alcohol is counterproductive when used with Clonidine and with Dicyclomine, which is used to relieve abdominal cramps. Ask your doctor about using alcohol to help you sleep — he will most likely prescribe something for you. Neither of you should be concerned that you will become addicted to sleeping pills with the amount that he'll prescribe. Plus, it is very difficult to become dependent upon Temazepam, anyway.

Loperamide HCl (Imodium) should be prescribed for diarrhea, although you can also buy this over the counter. Dicyclomine is prescribed for abdominal cramps. Dicyclomine, like Clonidine, may make you drowsy, which, given the circumstances, is not a bad thing. Finally, you should get acetaminophen for muscle aches.

With these five drugs, you are in a pretty good position to detox. Check the instructions for each drug carefully and write out a schedule. In general, you should put yourself on a six hour schedule. If you have a large habit, every six hours take: 0.1 mg Clonidine, 10 mg Librium, 2 mg Loperamide, 20 mg Dicyclomine, and 600 mg of acetaminophen. Hold to this schedule for three full days and then start to liberalize it. After three days, your body should be returning to normal. You definitely should not need as much Clonidine as before; after six days you should stop taking Clonidine altogether. The longest lasting physical symptom of withdrawal is usually insomnia, but you should not take your sleeping pills for more than ten days. Take the other medications as needed. If you are still experiencing nausea, diarrhea, or muscle aches after two weeks you should consult a doctor.

If you cannot or will not see a doctor about your detox, it is possible to get the drugs that you need by yourself. Particularly if you just want the Clonidine, this is relatively easy to do. When pharmacies get prescriptions for opioids or Valium-like drugs, they are more uptight because these are "drugs of abuse." But Clonidine is not a drug that is thought to be used recreationally, so little thought will be given to a prescription. Even a small prescription of benzodiazepines will not likely raise a red flag when coupled with the other drugs you need — the pharmacist will know what you are up to, though.

You have three options if you want to get your medication without a doctor: two involve faking prescriptions and one involves Mexico. The first is to steal some prescription forms from your doctor when you go to see him. These days, with computers, even this is unnecessary. It is possible to reproduce these forms if you get a single copy (probably from some previous prescription). Faking the handwriting is the easy part of this process. The hard part is knowing what to write. Sad as it is to say, most doctors do not know the scientific names of the drugs they prescribe — instead, they know the brand names. But this isn't always the case. Clonidine is usually prescribed as "Clonidine HCl 0.1 mg Tablets." Loperamide will be called "Imodium 2 mg Capsules." Dicyclomine is "Bentyl 20 mg Tablets." And Librium is "Librium 10 mg Capsules." In all prescriptions, make sure that you include quantities. Thirty of everything is pretty common.

The second option is to telephone the prescription in. Most medical office staff are female, so if you are male, you do best to have a girlfriend call it in. "Hi, this is Barbara from Dr. Thiel's office. I have a prescription for Dotty Wilson. Let's see here, 30 Bentyl 20 mg tablets..." And so on. It is imperative that whoever calls sound upbeat and professional; if the caller sounds at all high (e.g., slurred or very slow speech), you'll get caught. Also bear in mind that they may ask you questions about the prescription. Some will be easy. If they ask you, for example, if generics are alright, they are, because it will save you a small fortune. But some questions will be technical. For this reason, you should read up on all the drugs you are requesting and have a pill handbook close by.

If you choose to fake prescriptions, understand that it is very illegal. You can get caught (people do all the time). If you are, you'll be sent to jail and probably end up in a drug treatment program. It is a lot easier to find an out-of-town doctor and get regular prescriptions. Some doctors have ethical problems with this because they believe that addicts should only be detoxed under supervision. If you run into such a doctor, ask for a referral to a doctor who doesn't have such a problem. Doctors with such "ethical concerns" (they're usually just control freaks) don't actually care about you. They just don't want you on their minds — sending you to another doctor eliminates this problem.

Your final option is legal, but it takes work. In 1988 the Food and Drug Administration ruled that it was legal for individuals to import drugs for their own personal use. There are two criteria: first, the drugs must be regarded as safe in the country from which they originate and second, the quantity must not be greater than a three month supply. Of critical importance to us is that Clonidine may be purchased over the counter in Mexico. So you may have a Mexican pharmacy ship you Clonidine without fuss. The only possible wrinkle is that you are supposed to have a doctor who is overseeing your care. This will only be a problem if the U.S. Customs should seize your package — this is highly unlikely. Should this happen, however, you will receive a form letter asking for a signed statement that you are buying the drugs for personal use along with some other information including the name of your doctor. If this should happen, you may need to get a doctor. A related method of getting drugs is to physically go to Mexico and either stay there or bring drugs back with you.

Cold Turkey

There are only a few things that need to be said about this form of detox. The most important is that it is time honored: junkies have been detoxing in this way for hundreds, if not thousands of years. They survived, and so will you. If you have a small habit, then you might not experience a great deal of pain. Kicking a big habit in this manner can feel like hell on earth. One cold turkey withdrawal I lived through saw me sitting on the toilet, wrapped in a quilt. Sweat was pouring off me, but I was freezing cold, shivering violently. I was experiencing liquid diarrhea which was acidic; my anus was on fire. Every few minutes I would projectile vomit into the sink beside me. Remembering moments like these are very helpful in staying clean.

There will be at least 24 hours during which you will not want to be far from a toilet. Even with this proximity, you should really acquire some kind of adult size diaper. The reason is simple:

sometimes you will not make it in time. You should also carry around some kind of bowl with you. Diarrhea and vomiting can come on quite suddenly and they can be quite violent. You don't want to be caught unprepared. Also, you don't want to hurt yourself in some desperate lunge for the bathroom.

You must drink lots of fluids during your detox even if you are convinced that you just vomit it all back up. The fact is that some of the water does get absorbed into your system and you need it. The only way that detox is going to kill you is by dehydrating you. Make sure that you do not drink diuretics: alcohol or anything with caffeine in it. It is best to drink things that will replenish your electrolytes. Gatorade or PowerAde, or any similar drink will do nicely.

Whenever you can manage it, try to eat something. You will lose a lot of energy with all of the fluids you are giving up and replenishing it will help you, even though it may not seem like it at the time. A time-honored diet for detoxing junkies is orange juice and chocolate bars. About the only thing that I have been able to stomach during detox has been Nilla Wafers. I would stick with relatively bland foods: Ramen Noodles and chicken broth are good choices. When you get there, you'll know what sounds palatable.

When all is said and done, the worst thing about this kind of detox is that you will get very little sleep. If you can, get a TV, VCR, and about 30 movies that you really want to see. This will help the time pass. Books may sound like a good idea but most of the time you will be so exhausted (but still unable to sleep), that you won't be up to reading. And don't depend upon cable to save you if you don't have premium channels — everything on while you're detoxing will suck.[1] One time when I detoxed I subscribed to every pay station there was. It was easy to justify, too: I was kicking a $100 per day habit — what was $50 a month for cable? This is a good way to look at your detox; there are few things you can buy that even a small habit wouldn't quickly eat up.

---

[1] Actually, everything will suck. You will be very unhappy because your body is not used to producing endorphins (you've been feeding your body endorphins in the form of heroin). You will think the world is a very gray, awful place. Give it time; you won't always feel that way.

I wish that I could describe the detox cycle but I can't. Everyone is different, both in the timing of the symptoms and in the symptoms that are experienced. Remember the symptoms of detox: depression, insomnia, nausea, vomiting, diarrhea, abdominal and other muscle cramps, anxiety, irritability, watery eyes, general body aches, restlessness, perspiration, dilated pupils, 'goose flesh,' hot flashes, gagging, fever, increased heart rate, increased blood pressure, dehydration, weight loss, nervousness, hyperactivity, leg cramps, and alternating profuse sweating and chills. I have simply never felt some of these symptoms, but don't be surprised if you feel them all, at one time or another. The main thing is to know that they are part of the detox, they are cyclical, and that the cycle will end.

After two or three days, you will start to feel better. While you are going through the process, just keep reminding yourself that the pain will pass and that you will eventually be in a much more pleasant place than you have been. Five days really isn't that long.

Detoxing Yourself

You can detox yourself with opioid substitution, non-opioid medication, or nothing at all. Regardless of how you detox yourself, there are practical matters with which you must deal. By planning ahead you greatly reduce the pain that you will experience — even with a cold turkey withdrawal — thereby greatly increasing your chances of successfully eliminating your addiction.

Find a Good Location

The first thing you must do if you want to detox yourself is find a good location. This usually involves going out of town. The reason is simple: you will experience some discomfort and if heroin is readily available, you will most likely use it because, after all, you can always detox later. A time-honored location is a farm. But any remote location will work. You may also rent a hotel room, but it should either have a kitchenette or room service.

Get a Caretaker

The second thing you should do, but probably the first thing you will do, is to find someone to take care of you. You don't have to do this — many people have detoxed all by themselves. But having someone around has many advantages. First, you will not be feeling your best — whether this is because of withdrawal symptoms or a lack of sleep or all the drugs you are taking to mask the withdrawal symptoms does not matter. It is very nice to have someone around to help out.

A caretaker can take responsibility for giving you medication when it is time, making sure that you drink lots of fluids, and encouraging you to eat. They can also get medical attention in the event of an emergency. They can provide some kind of connection to the real world and give you a reason to keep going. Finally, a caretaker can stop you from going out to score — you'd be surprised how capable a withdrawing junkie can be when it comes to getting heroin.

Plan Ahead

Plan ahead. Try to get everything that you need for your detox before you begin. This is particularly true if you are alone. But even when you aren't, a helper has often come back from a shopping trip to an empty house — the junkie using the opportunity to go out and score. But even still, when a caretaker leaves, he is not able to take care of you. So try to have everything you need ahead of time: drugs, food, drinks (no caffeine and alcohol), and entertainment (usually music and videos).

Other Things

There are several things that you can do which may make your detox happier or at least more bearable. Think about them before you begin so that you can make plans to integrate them.

Acupuncture

Many people find acupuncture helpful. Don't listen to any of the garbage that acupuncturists will tell you — things like, "acupuncture has been proven to help in detox." Maybe it does help and maybe it doesn't — it certainly hasn't been proven. What has been proven is that acupuncture helps in blocking and managing pain. So if you go to an acupuncturist, let him put all the needles he wants into your ears, but have him also give you a pain treatment. Tell him what you are feeling and find out what he would recommend for a person who wasn't a drug addict who came to him with those symptoms.

Yoga

The main help that I have experienced from acupuncture comes from the fact that it makes me sit still for a little while. This brings me to something that I have found very helpful: yoga. Especially with all of the muscle pain that you will feel during detox, light yoga can really help. If you don't know yoga it is basically stretching combined with a little meditation: stretch to some position, hold it, and try to clear your mind. If you feel up to it, you will likely find that it does take away some of your muscle pain in addition to improving your mood and generally making you feel better.

Exercise

A little light exercise can do a world of good. Mostly, this will involve little more than a walk around the block — if that. If you feel up to it, try to take your walk outside. You'll be surprised how much you like the outdoors after being shut inside for a few days.

Marijuana

Finally, I'd like to make a pitch for a drug I really don't like: marijuana. Nausea is one of the primary withdrawal symptoms and marijuana really does help alleviate nausea. Marijuana can also be helpful with insomnia. On the other hand, if you have bad reactions to marijuana, it will likely only make your detox worse, so stay away. But it can be an effective tool for detox, especially if you enjoy its effects.

Keep Going

Try to complete your detox. Most people quit their detox right when things are about to get better (not surprisingly, this is also when things are at their worst). Remember that you aren't that far away from success and your intense desire to make it end is actually a good sign. And if you quit now, you will just have to go through all of this pain again. On the other hand, if you have to quit, quit. Especially if you're trying to do a cold turkey withdrawal —after all, it may have been very educational. Now you can appreciate what a medicated detox actually does for you.

Most of all, don't beat yourself up if you can't detox yourself. It took me many tries to get it right. Even under the best of circumstances, it is not pleasant to go through detox. You can always try again. Look at any detox as a learning experience: it will teach you how to improve future attempts and it will teach you a lot about what to look for when hiring someone else to detox you.

Staying Clean

There is a saying about heroin: getting off is easy, it's staying off that's hard. There is much truth in this saying. Just the same, much of the truth comes from the fact that addicts are rarely given any tools to help them stay clean other than the admonition to "go to NA meetings." The implicit message is that all your pain and suffering is in your head. But this is not the case.

Antidepressants

I highly recommend that you get yourself a prescription for a serotonin re-uptake inhibitor (e.g., Paxil, Zoloft) — these drugs are commonly referred to as "antidepressants," but in fact there are different kinds of antidepressants and not all affect serotonin. The lack of heroin in your system causes your serotonin levels to get all out of kilter and antidepressants help modulate your serotonin levels and get your serotonin production and uptake mechanisms working properly again. This is assuming that they were working properly in the first place. Many people become addicted to heroin because of serotonin problems. Start taking antidepressants at the beginning of your detox (or even a few days before), and continue taking them for at least three months. You may want to discuss getting off them with your doctor, but bear in mind that most doctors are highly resistant to taking people off them. But you should give it a try. Being forced to take any drug sucks — isn't this why you just detoxed yourself from heroin?

Anxiety is common to the recently clean. Doctors often treat anxiety with antidepressants, but if you are experiencing extreme levels, you should try an anti-anxiety drug such as Buspar. Note, however, that Buspar can have many side effects including, ironically, anxiety. It is also a pain to take; usually you are asked to take 5 mg three times per day. Despite this, it is a Godsend for many people and it is worth checking out.

Natural Medicine and Food

In addition to drugs, there are many things that can help you stay clean. Acupuncture is helpful to many. You might try yoga and meditation. Eating a healthy diet couldn't hurt and the same goes for taking vitamins.

Support Groups

Many people find NA and similar groups very helpful in staying off drugs. Even I, with my jaundiced views, find NA meetings occasionally helpful and even inspiring. The good side is that you get to meet and commiserate with a lot of people who are in many ways like you. The bad side is that it can make you as obsessed about drugs as you ever were when you were using. I have left NA meetings craving heroin far more than when I showed up. So use them or don't, depending upon whether they work for you or not.

There are a few good ideas that you'll hear at NA meetings. One is that you need to distance yourself from your drug-using friends. This is true to an extent. What you really need to do is distance yourself from your drug-*abusing* friends. Your friends who use drugs responsibly demonstrate the kind of behavior that you want to emulate — even if you don't want to use again. Plus, do you really want to spend the rest of your life around nothing but ex-drug addicts (clean though they may be)? Don't limit yourself. Being clean means you can enjoy life and people are one of the great joys of life.

If you live in a large city in the United States you will probably have access to S.M.A.R.T. (Self Management And Recovery Training), Recovery, or Rational Recovery meetings. In my opinion, these meetings have all the advantages of NA with fewer drawbacks. First, they teach that you do have power over your addiction and that you can use that power to change your addictive behavior. Second, they teach that going to meetings is a temporary measure to get over your addiction rather than a life-long commitment — exchanging dependence on drugs for dependence on a group. Third, and I think most important, they teach that you can get better — you don't have to spend the rest of your life in self-flagellation.

Find a New Life

By far the best thing you can do for yourself is to get a new life. You cannot continue with your old life because it now has this big hole in it where heroin used to reside. Now is the time to start making changes to your life in the areas that got you addicted in the first place. In drug therapy I was asked if I understood that avoiding addiction required not getting high at all. I responded that the only way I knew to stay off drugs was to get high — in all those ways that one does so without using drugs. If you think that staying off drugs is about depriving yourself, then you will not succeed at staying off drugs. You've got to get happy. Find things that make you happy and do them. That's what life is all about anyway.

Going Back

Don't let the dogma fool you: just because you became addicted to heroin does not necessarily mean that you can never use heroin responsibly — though it may. There are many factors that go into making someone a heroin addict: biological, psychological, and sociological. Under the right circumstances, anyone can become addicted to heroin. This should act as a warning to the non-addict, but also encouragement to the addict.

Once you quit heroin, you need to stay off of it for a long enough time that you won't simply fall into the old patterns which led you to your addiction before. If you started using heroin every day because of a failed relationship, I'll bet that you still aren't over that relationship. I'll bet it will take you a long time to forget all your pager numbers. I'll bet the street dealers will still be working the same areas at the same times for a while. If you are in physical pain because of some condition, I'll bet heroin hasn't done a thing to fix the problem. It will take a while for your life to change. It might take a year. It might take ten years. But rest assured, it will take a lot longer than a week or a month.

If you go back after a short period of time, you are almost certainly fooling yourself. You really need time to create a whole new life. And under most circumstances, you will have done so much damage to your life that you will have a lot of work to do. Just on the simplest level, you've probably neglected your friends and family. Take some time to remember what life was like without heroin. After you've done that, maybe you'll be able to make heroin a part of your life again and not allow it to take over your life.

Chapter Eight
Parting Words

I have deeply mixed feelings about heroin: some days I think it's just the greatest thing in the world, and some days I think people are crazy to even consider trying it. In contemplative moments, I suppose the reality is somewhere in between.

The law is to blame, of course. Without it, most people would be perfectly satisfied with drinking a little opium tea at night to relax. The college kids would throw back a couple ounces of morphine and get naked with each other. And the addicts would be sucking morphine down all day long and smoking heroin to get high at night. It wouldn't be a perfect world, but it would be a better world.

But we can't ignore the law because it affects the heroin user in so many ways: price, quality, disease, and jail. Wouldn't it just be easier to do a far more dangerous, but legal, drug like alcohol? Of course it would. If an easy life is what you want, why would you even think of using heroin? People use heroin to make their lives better, and they think that heroin will make their lives better.

But there are consequences that heroin users must accept. You may think that you accept these consequences, but that's mostly because they are not staring you in the face. You might have second thoughts about your heroin use when you're standing half-naked against a wall with an assault rifle pointed at your face after a military unit has just busted into your house. This isn't just some hypothetical situation — it happens to people all the time. Of course, it doesn't really matter what illegal drug you're using or even if you are using illegal drugs at all. But as a heroin user, you are more likely to experience this than if you were, say, a marijuana smoker.

On the other hand, heroin can be heaven on earth. I think a majority of people would go through the pain that I have gone through in order to experience the overwhelming joy that I once got from heroin. For the right person, there is nothing that could even approach the effects of this drug.

As I sit here writing this, my involvement with heroin is over. I've lived its good side and I've lived its bad side — but even without the good side, I'm glad that I was involved with heroin. I learned a great deal from the experience and when I finally landed free of heroin, I found that I had touched down at a better place than the place I was when I first started using. But I understand that I could have as easily ended up dead.

Whether you use heroin and how responsibly you use it will depend upon your desires. If you follow the guidelines found in this book, you will make your heroin involvement safer and happier. But that doesn't mean that you won't still end up in jail or sick from some awful disease or even dead. Using heroin is a dangerous activity — knowledge only makes it less so.

The worst thing about writing this book is that I know I will be attacked for writing it, just as surely as I know that this information is necessary and that it will save lives and make the world a better place. Whenever something goes wrong — especially something like a drug-related death — people look around desperately for something or someone to blame. I have this horrible vision of some guy dying of a heroin overdose, and when the family members are cleaning up, they find a copy of *The Heroin User's Handbook*. Suddenly, everything is clear. This guy didn't die because he chose to be involved in a dangerous activity or because the laws forced him to ingest junk instead of a pharmaceutical drug. No, he died because Francis Moraes, Ph.D., tricked him into it by providing information. Then come the lawsuits. Then come the call for such books to be banned. Then comes the vilification of me. On the other hand, had I written a book filled with lies about how horrible illegal drugs are,[1] I would make more money and no one would ever sue me for implicitly causing people to drink alcohol or smoke cigarettes.

Using heroin is a choice. I sincerely hope that any person who uses heroin will read this book. As I stated at the beginning of this book, I do not wish to encourage heroin use. But there is enough anti-drug propaganda out there — my poorly distributed thesis on heroin use could not possibly overpower the government's billion-dollar anti-drug campaign. My effort does have one advantage, though: I know that people make their own choices (the government thinks it can make choices for people), and by providing them with the most objective information available, I allow them to make the most well-informed decision possible.

People tell me that I have a savior complex. I suppose that this is true. But I don't see myself as Jesus Christ — I'm not trying to create a perfect world. I think of myself more like Moses — I just want my people to survive. With this in mind, I leave you with my Ten Commandments:

Ten Commandments of Responsible Heroin Use

1. Don't use with junkies.

2. Don't use more than three days in a row.

3. After using, don't use for twice as long as the time you used.

4. Don't share administration equipment.

5. Don't use in dirty places.

6. Don't mix heroin with alcohol.

---

[1] Here is an irony for you: most anti-drug books do a much worse job of vilifying heroin than I do in this book. In particular, such books tend to overstate how good the heroin high feels (usually ignoring or dismissing side-effects like nausea) and understate how bad withdrawal is.

7. Don't neglect your health.
8. Don't let non-users know that you use.
9. Always keep an active social life.
10. Don't get careless when scoring.

Whatever you do, be careful and have fun.

Appendix A
Glossary

Abuse: The USFDA defines abuse as "deliberately taking a substance for other than its intended purpose, and in a manner that can result in damage to the person's health or his ability to function."

Adatuss: Hydrocodone antitussive.

Administration: The means by which a drug is taken.

Adulteration: The process of diluting a drug.

Agonist: Any opioid that produces morphine-like or codeine-like effects on the body.

AIDS: Acquired Immune Deficiency Syndrome.

Alkaloid: A molecule that contains nitrogen, carbon, oxygen, and hydrogen. All opioids are alkaloids.

Alphaprodine: A short-acting morphine-like synthetic analgesic.

Analgesic: A drug which relieves pain without rendering the patient unconscious.

Anexsia-D: An analgesic soup in pill form, consisting of aspirin, caffeine, phenacetin, and Hydrocodone.

Anileridine: A synthetic opioid similar to Demerol.

Antagonist: A drug that blocks the effects of an opiate. They are used in cases of overdose and to show that a user is an addict — usually for the purpose of allowing him into a methadone program.

Antitussive: A drug that relieves coughing.

Apomorphine: A non-euphoric morphine derivative used to induce vomiting.

Artillery: See Works.

Back up: See Pull-Back.

Bag: A dose of heroin, usually between $10 and $20.

Balloon: This often refers to a single dose of heroin — usually an eighth gram. Heroin is often distributed in small balloons so that it can be stored in one's mouth and swallowed (without loss) should law enforcement appear.

Barbiturates: A class of sedative, hypnotic drugs which depress the central nervous system. The longer-acting barbiturates are removed by the kidneys; the short-acting ones are removed by the liver.

Beat: To cheat.

Benzodiazepines: A class of minor tranquilizers with lifetimes anywhere from a few hours to a few days. These are removed by the liver.

B & O Supprettes: An anal suppository containing powdered opium and belladonna extract.

Booting: Repeated flushing and pull-back when IV injecting. It is often said to be a means of prolonging the high, but seems more often to be mere play.

Bundle: Usually 20 bags of heroin, but it can vary.

Buprenorphine: A narcotic antagonist.

Butorphanol: A narcotic agonist/antagonist used as an analgesic.

Burn: To cheat.

Chasing the Dragon: Smoking heroin.

China White: White powder heroin from Asia — usually referring to heroin funneled through France. Not all white powder heroin is China White.

Chip: To use drugs in a non-addictive manner.

Chipper: A non-addicted, casual drug user.

Chiva: This actually means marijuana but for some reason, it means heroin in the US.

Cirrhosis: Chronic destruction of the liver.

Clonidine: A blood pressure medication that is highly effective at modulating opiate withdrawal symptoms.

Cocktail: A mixture of different drugs taken at once.

Cold Turkey: To detox off of heroin abruptly without medication.

Connection: Dealer.

Cooker: Spoon or other device used to cook heroin for injection.

Cop: To acquire drugs.

Cut: The act of diluting a drug. Also the substance with which a drug is diluted.

Cyclazocine: A narcotic antagonist.

Darvon: An analgesic soup containing propoxyphene.

Demerol: Brand name for Meperidine, a synthetic opiate similar to morphine, but only about as potent as codeine.

Dextromoramide: A very potent synthetic opiate.

Dihydrocodeine: A semisynthetic opiate similar to codeine.

Dihydromorphinone: Dilaudid.

Dilaudid: A semisynthetic opiate, about three times as potent as heroin.

Dime: $10.

Diphenoxylate: A mild semisynthetic opiate used as an antidiarrheic.

Dolene: An analgesic soup containing propoxyphene.

Dolophine Hydrochloride: Methadone.

Done: Slang for Methadone, as in "meth-a-*done*."(Note: it is not pronounced like the word "done," but rather with a long "o.")

Dysphoria: A withdrawal symptom that is distinguished by feelings of uneasiness and malaise.

Endorphins: Compounds produced by the body, which are used to regulate pain and create a sense of well-being. They are very similar and act in the same ways as opioids.

Enkephalins: Short-chain amino acids that act as opioids. They are a form of endorphins.

EMIT: An acronym for "enzyme multiplied immunoassay technique." It is a common system used for detecting drug use from urine samples.

Fentanyl: An extremely potent opioid, roughly 100 times as powerful as morphine.

Fit: Syringe.

Front: A loan of drugs.

GC/MS: Gas chromatographer/mass spectrometer. This is a device that is used for many valid applications. It can also be used to do drug screening tests. These tests are expensive, so employers and bureaucracies don't like to use them, but they are the only tests that are reasonably accurate (99.98%). They are also the only tests that can distinguish between morphine and a poppy-seed bagel.

Gimmick: Syringe.

Golden Crescent: An important area in the production of opium. It encompasses Pakistan, Iran, and Afghanistan.

Golden Triangle: An important area in the production of opium. It encompasses Thailand, northern Laos, and eastern Burma.

Hepatitis: Inflammation of the liver.

Heroin Slang: First, I'll give you the words I've actually heard. Brown, black tar, China White, Chiva, dope, H, horse, junk, Mexican, rock, scag, scar, shit, smack, tar, white. I've collected a number of slang terms from books. Some of these are so silly that I sometimes wonder if a playful junkie wasn't just pulling some clueless sociologist's leg: big H, blanco, blanks, boy, brother, brown sugar, caballo, ca-ca (counterfeit), cat, chick, Chinese red, cobics, crap, cura, dogie, doojee (duji), flea powder, goods, hard stuff, Harry (hairy), Henry, joy powder, ka-ka, Mexican mud, poison, red chicken, schmeck, snow, stuff, sugar, tecata, thing, white stuff.

Hit: To inject.

Hycodan: An antitussive containing hydrocodone mixed with homatropine methylbromide.

Hycomine: An antitussive containing hydrocodone mixed with phenylpropanolamine.

Hydrocodone: A codeine derivative, which is roughly six times as potent. It has the same chemical formula as codeine, but a different geometrical structure.

Hydromorphone: Dilaudid.

Hypnotic: A drug that induces sleep.

Hypodermic: Syringe.

Imodium: The antidiarrheic medication Loperamide.

IV: Intravenous.

Jones: A desire for heroin.

Joypopper: Chipper.

Kick: Withdraw.

Kit: Works.

LAAM: Levo-alpha-acetylmethadol. It is a synthetic opiate with a three day halflife, which has been used instead of methadone in maintenance programs.

Laudanum: A tincture of opium.

LD50: Lethal dose in 50% of the sample.

Levallorphan: A narcotic antagonist.

Levo-Dromoran: This is basically pure levorphanol in pill or injectable form.

Levorphanol: A long-acting synthetic opiate with fewer side effects than morphine.

Lomotil: An antidiarrheic containing the synthetic opiate diphenoxylate.

Loperamide: An non-euphoric opioid that can be used in detox.

Lorfan: Levallorphan.

Mainline: Intravenous injection.

Mark: A person who is easily tricked or cheated.

Meperidine: A synthetic opiate commonly known as Demerol.

Methadone: A synthetic opiate with a long halflife.

MPTP: A "designer drug" with effects similar to morphine, but can produce permanent symptoms resembling those of Parkinson's disease.

Nalbuphine: A narcotic agonist/antagonist.

Nalorphine: A narcotic antagonist derived from morphine.

Naloxone: A narcotic antagonist.

Naltrexone: A narcotic antagonist.

Narcan: Naloxone.

Numorphan: Oxymorphone.

Noscapine: An opium alkaloid used as an antitussive.

OD: Overdose.

One and one: Heroin and cocaine sold together in a single bag.

Opiates: Technically, morphine and codeine and any drugs derived from them. It is often used to refer to any substance with opium-like effects.

Opioids: Synthetic opium-like drugs.

Opium: The dried juice from an unripe seed pod of the flower *Papaver somniferum*. The word "opium" is thrown around very loosely, but the definition is very specific.

Oxycodone: A semisynthetic morphine derivative, about half as potent.

Oxymorphone: A semisynthetic morphine derivative, about ten times as potent.

Outfit: Syringe.

Pantopon: Quite literally, opium in a syringe. This contains all of the alkaloids of opium in a purified form. It is no longer produced.

Papaverine: A non-euphoric alkaloid of opium, which is widely used in the creation of semisynthetic opiates.

Paraphernalia: Works.

Paregoric: An opium tincture with a high alcohol content.

Parenteral: Pertaining to injection in any of its many forms.

Pentazocine: A mild narcotic antagonist, which is also an analgesic.

Percocet: Oxycodone mixed with Acetaminophen.

Percodan: Oxycodone mixed with Aspirin.

Propoxyphene: A synthetic opiate, which is the primary ingredient of Darvon.

Pull-back: Pulling the syringe plunger back so that the syringe will fill with blood if the needle is inside of a vein.

Pusher: A drug dealer. This is a misnomer based on the idea that dealers get users started.

Quinine: A bitter tasting alkaloid commonly used to cut heroin.

RIA: Radioimmunoassay. It is a common system used for detecting drug use from urine samples.

Roll: When a vein moves to the side as it is being injected into so that the needle does not enter the vein.

Roxicodone: Unadulterated oxycodone.

Rig: Syringe.

Run: A period of constant use. With heroin, this is generally a period of time addicted.

Score: To acquire drugs.

Script: A prescription.

Sedative: A drug that depresses the central nervous system and causes drowsiness.

Shoot up: Inject.

Skin pop: Subcutaneous (under the skin) injection.

Slam: To inject, especially intravenously.

Sniff: To inhale a liquid or solid through the nose.

Snort: To inhale a liquid or solid through the nose.

Speedball: This is heroin and cocaine mixed.

Stadol: A narcotic agonist/antagoinst used as an analgesic.

Step on: To mix a drug with an inert substance to make it seem to be a larger amount — the same as cut.

Straight: A non-drug-using person.

Strung out: Addicted to heroin.

Subcutaneous: The layer of blood vessels just under the skin.

Sublimaze: Fentanyl.

Syringe slang: Fit, gimmick, hypodermic, outfit, rig, works.

Talwin: Pentazocine.

Taste: An archaic method of determining the purity of white powder heroin. With it, the user literally tastes a small amount of the drug — if it is bitter, the sample is assumed to be fairly pure. It fell out of use when the bitter tasting alkaloid quinine became a widely used adulterant. A "taste" can also be a small amount.

Thebaine: An alkaloid of opium used to make several narcotic antagonists as well as codeine.

Tie: Tourniquet.

Tracks: Repeated needle entry scars along a vein.

Tussionex: An antitussive that contains hydrocodone.

Vicodin: A medication widely used for moderate pain, which contains hydrocodone and acetaminophen.

Works: A syringe or other device for administering heroin into a vein.

Appendix B
Recommended Reading

The following list of books would make a good "heroin library." This list is far from complete, however, and it is not limited to books about drugs. If you want to study heroin further, these books will give you a good start.

Avoiding Drugs

Introduction to Giving Up Drugs:
How to Get Off Drugs, by Ira Mothner and Alan Weitz (Simon & Schuster, Inc., New York, 1984). You will find a lot of interesting material on getting and staying off drugs in this book, but be aware of its conservative assumptions about drug addiction. It is still a good book to read.

Heroin Addiction Research:
Heroin Addiction: Theory, Research, and Treatment, by Jerome J. Platt (R. E. Krieger Publishing Company, Malabar, Florida, 1986). Platt has written three heroin addiction books (at last count). He believes far too much in methadone maintenance for any junkie's good. But this book provides an excellent overview of the literature on the issue of heroin addiction. Be careful to note the facts in the book and be careful of the conclusions,

which are not always justified by the facts. This is important when analyzing any scientific work.

Non-12-Step Drug Treatment:

The Small Book: A Revolutionary Alternative to Overcoming Drug and Alcohol Dependence, by Jack Trimpey (Dell Publishing, New York, 1992). Trimpey presents a rational approach to getting past drug addiction. Unlike NA, there is a scientific basis for Rational Recovery. If you feel the need for a support system, start with Rational Recovery or SMART Recovery. I recommend NA to people as the step before methadone maintenance.

Scientific Discussion of Addiction:

Diseasing of America: Addiction Treatment Out of Control, by Stanton Peele (D. C. Heath and Company, Lexington, Massachusetts, 1989). This book blows the lid off the idea that addiction is a disease. It can be very helpful in putting drug addiction into perspective and making you feel less like some sick creature who will always walk around with a monkey on his back.

Social Drug Use:

Drug, Set, and Setting: The Basis For Controlled Intoxicant Use, by Norman Earl Zinberg (Yale University Press, New Haven, 1984). When I first discovered Zinberg's work, I felt that I had been vindicated. Many people had told me that it was impossible to use heroin casually. Zinberg shows that there were many such users. He also shows what users do in order to control their use.

Drugs

Overview of Drugs:

Licit & Illicit Drugs, by Edward M. Brecher and the Editors of Consumer Reports (Little, Brown and Company, Boston, 1972). This book has a lot of good history in it and it debunks the idea that heroin is a dangerous drug. Just the same, the authors believe that "once an addict, always an addict" and so recommend methadone maintenance. Remember that when this book was written, no one had really studied ex-addicts. So all of the data came from the very worst addicts who, not surprisingly, were destined to continue on in their addiction. Other than this issue, however, this is a wonderful book.

Mail-order Drugs:

Smart Drugs & Nutrients, by Ward Dean and Morgenthaler (B&J Publications, Santa Cruz, CA, 1991) and *How To Buy Almost Any Drug Legally Without A Prescription*, by James H. Johnson (Avon Books, New York, 1990). These books are the best references for obtaining drugs from other countries. They have a lot of fluff though — descriptions of a lot of drugs that you won't be interested in. But they provide a good overview of the law that will most likely keep you out of trouble. One of the most important things you will find is that you have more options if you physically carry drugs into the country than you do when mail-ordering.

Pill Information:

Physician's Desk Reference, 53rd Edition, by Ronald Arky and others (Medical Economics Company, Montvale, NJ, 1999). This is the standard "pill" book. You may find others more readable, but if you are technically minded, this is the one to get. Unfortunately or fortunately, it is heavily steeped in the industry's emphasis on brand names and product manufacturers. There are a lot of reference works about pills — shop around and find the one that works for you.

Heroin Introduction:

The Little Book of Heroin, by Francis Moraes (Ronin Publishing, Inc, Berkeley, CA, 2000). This book is an overview of heroin rather than a user's guide. As such, it has more information about the science of heroin. It makes a good companion to *The Heroin User's Handbook*, but there is much overlap.

Opium Introduction:

Opium for the Masses, by Jim Hogshire (Loompanics Unlimited, Port Townsend, WA, 1994). Hogshire provides an excellent introduction to the opiates. This will be of interest to anyone interested in heroin.

More Opium:

The Little Book of Opium, by Francis Moraes and Debra Kita (Ronin Publishing, Inc, Berkeley, CA, 2001). This book gives a lot more information about the science of opium than Hogshire's book. It has detailed discussions of cultivation and pharmacology. It is an excellent companion to the Hogshire book.

Cocaine Introduction:

Cocaine Handbook: An Essential Reference, by David Lee (And/Or Press, Inc., Berkeley, California, 1981). This is the closest thing I've found to the present book, but for cocaine. If you are using cocaine, this is a good book to have. But note that it is still anti-drug use.

Drug Encyclopedia:

The Encyclopedia of Drug Abuse, Second Edition, by Robert O'Brien, Sidney Cohen, Glen Evans, and James Fine (Facts On File, New York, 1992). This book is really good to have if you want to be able to find out what a drug does (and so forth), but only if you aren't intimidated by more scientific works. There is a lot of information packed into this book. The only down side can be seen in its title: Drug Abuse. The authors think that drug use is bad but this does not affect their science which is mostly first rate.

Selected Heroin Research:

"It's So Good, Don't Even Try It Once": Heroin in Perspective, edited by David E. Smith (Prentice-Hall, Englewood Cliffs, New Jersey, 1972). This is a collection of essays about heroin. It all focuses around the 1970 heroin scene, but it provides some interesting insights into the many aspects of heroin use.

History

The History of Heroin:
The Birth of Heroin and the Demonization of the Dope Fiend, by Th. Metzger (Loompanics Unlimited, Port Townsend, WA, 1998). This is an excellent history of the opiates which dispels many myths and explains how we got to our current, troubling cultural situation.

The History of the Most Recent Drug War:
Drug Warriors and Their Prey: From Police Power to Police State, by Richard Lawrence Miller (Praeger, Westport, Connecticut, 1996). This book is so frightening and accurate that it will make you want to leave the country. It is a perceptive look at how illegal drug users are treated in the United States and why they are treated so.

Medicine

Introduction to Disease:
Merck Manual of Medical Information: Home Edition, edited by Robert Berkow (Merck Research Laboratories, Whitehouse Station, NJ, 1997). This is the best disease book I've found. It is detailed and inexpensive.

Heroin Specific Medicine:
Medical Readings on Heroin, by Oliver E. Byrd and Thomas R. Byrd (Boyd & Fraser Publishing Company, 1972). This is a collection of summaries of medical papers on heroin use and abuse. It is old, but it still contains most of the important information on diseases related to heroin use.

Medical Procedures:
The Lippincott Manual of Nursing Practice, Sixth Edition, by Sandra M. Nettina, et al. (Lippincott-Raven Publishers, Philadelphia, 1996). Truthfully, this book is a bit much. It contains far more information than you would ever need, but there is no better source for information on the proper procedures for things

like intravenous injection. You might try looking for simpler (and smaller and cheaper) nursing texts — these may suit you as well.

Miscellaneous

Getting Along:
The Evolution of Cooperation, by Robert Axelrod (Basic Books, New York, 1984). This book makes an intriguing argument for the Golden Rule. It shows that in the long run, you are better off treating others fairly than trying to screw them. And this is based entirely on self-interest — there is no government or church to enforce this outcome.

Deceiving Others:
The Trick Brain, by Dariel Fitzkee (Lee Jacobs Productions, Pomeroy, OH, 1989). In this book, Fitzkee teaches magic from a theoretical standpoint. From a layperson's standpoint there is really no other book If you wish to learn the art of deception — either because you wish to be a magician, a card shark, or you simply wish to beat a drug test — get this book.

Dressing Conservatively:
John T. Molloy's New Dress for Success, by John T. Molloy. (Warner Books, New York, 1988) and *The Woman's Dress for Success Book*, by John T. Molloy (Follett Publishing Company, Chicago, 1977). Molloy teaches the reader how to dress well, but conservatively. This information is not only of use in court. In general, cops will be less inclined to think that you are up to no good if you are dressed in a "business uniform." Even if you dress well, his books are very useful, because of the style considerations.

Law

Dealing with Cops:
A Speeder's Guide to Avoiding Tickets, by James M. Eagan (Avon Books, New York, 1990). No other book provides the kinds of

insights into the motivations of cops as this book. Perhaps it is because the author was a cop, but Eagan pulls no punches. Although the book is overall pro-cop, it is a very worthwhile read.

How Cops Relate:

Thinking Cop, Feeling Cop, by Stephen M. Hennessy (Leadership Inc. Publishing, Scottsdale, Arizona, 1992). This guy seems to think that cops are just ordinary people, so he has applied normal psychology to them. This is very useful, but I think more insights would be gained by applying abnormal psychology.

Introduction to the Criminal Justice System:

You Are Going To Prison, by Jim Hogshire (Loompanics Unlimited, Port Townsend, WA, 1994). There is no doubt that every heroin user should own and study this book. It guides you through the process of being arrested right through to frying in the electric chair. I wish I had read this book before I had my legal problems.

Drug Law:

Controlled Substances: Chemical & Legal Guide to Federal Drug Laws, by Alexander T. Shulgin (Ronin Publishing, Inc, Berkeley, CA, 1992). This book is a little out of date, but there is no other book like it. It lays down the U.S. drug laws in a clear and coherent manner.

Psychology

Physiological Types:

Please Understand Me: Character & Temperament Types, by David Keissey and Marilyn Bates (Promethean Nemesis, Del Mar, California, 1984). This book provides a very readable introduction to the theory of psychological types. It will give you a useful model that you can apply to interactions with other humans (and cops).

You Will Also Want to Read:

❑ **85186 OPIUM FOR THE MASSES: A Practical Guide to Growing Poppies and Making Opium,** *by Jim Hogshire.* Everything you ever wanted to know about the beloved poppy and its amazing properties, including: What does the opium high feel like?; The stunning similarities between opium and your body's natural endorphins; Morphine and its derivatives; How to grow opium poppies; Sources for fertile poppy seeds; And much more! Also includes rare photographs and detailed illustrations. *1994, 5½ x 8½, 112 pp, illustrated, soft cover.* $14.95.

❑ **40083 YOU ARE GOING TO PRISON,** *by Jim Hogshire.* This is the most accurate, no-bullshit guide to prison life we have ever seen. Topics covered include: custody; prison; jailhouse justice; execution and more. When are public defenders your best options? What was Mike Tyson's second biggest mistake? How do you stay on the good side of the guards and other prisoners? If you or a loved one is about to be swallowed up by the system, you need this information if you hope to come out whole. *1994, 5½ x 8½, 185 pp, indexed, soft cover.* $14.95.

❑ **85203 STONED FREE, How To Get High Without Drugs,** *by Patrick Wells and Douglas Rushkoff.* Now you can say "NO!" to drugs and get high anyway! This book enumerates many drugless consciousness-altering techniques, both timeless and recent in origin, that anyone can make use of. Meditation, breathing techniques, high-tech highs, sleep and dream manipulation, and numerous other methods are examined in detail. Avoid incarceration, save money, and skip the wear and tear on your body, while getting higher than a kite. *1995, 5½ x 8½, 157 pp, illustrated, soft cover.* $14.95.

❑ **85212 THE POLITICS OF CONSCIOUSNESS,** *by Steve Kubby with a Foreword by Terence McKenna.* The War on Drugs is really a war on freedom of thought. Our fundamental right to pursuit of happiness includes the innate right to explore inner space without government interference. Author Steve Kubby explains how the authorities have short-circuited democracy through illegal, unconstitutional sanctions on the use of psychoactive plants and substances... and voices a fiercely patriotic rallying cry for a campaign of liberation that will enable us to recapture our freedom to think as we choose. This is a compelling, brutally honest book that is unlike anything ever published before. *1995, 8½ x 11, 160 pp, illustrated, soft cover.* $18.95.

☐ **85346 HERBS OF THE NORTHERN SHAMAN, A Guide to Mind-Altering Plants of the Northern Hemisphere,** *by Steve Andrews.* This book describes in clear, understandable terms the plants and fungi, their active constituents, the dosages, and their effects on the human mind and body. Whether you are an explorer of alternative realities or a botany buff and consummate student this book is for you. *2000, 8½ x 11, 116 pp, illustrated, indexed, soft cover.* $14.95.

☐ **94317 SEX, DRUGS, & THE TWINKIE MURDERS,** *by Paul Krassner.* The "Zen Bastard" rides again! In this brand-new collection of satirical pieces, Paul Krassner, America's sharpest and funniest social commentator lets fly at everything from sex and drugs to the Twinkie murders. More than 40 pieces are included, all of them demonstrating why Paul Krassner ought to be declared a National Resource. *2000, 5½ x 8½, 368 pp, soft cover.* $19.95.

☐ **85293 DRINK AS MUCH AS YOU WANT AND LIVE LONGER, The Intelligent Person's Guide to Healthy Drinking,** *by Frederick M. Beyerlein, MBA, MS, CNSD, RD.* Let's face it, most people drink. Some drink casually, while others drink uncontrollably. The fact is that alcohol can be bad for your health. There are hangovers, liver damage, beer guts, not to mention mental issues. That's why author/nutritionist, Frederick M. Beyerlein wrote this book. Sure, it may be controversial, but the fact is if you are going to drink, do it in a healthier manner. By following Beyerlein's system, readers will never again experience the illustrious hangover! Readers will soon learn how to protect their livers by eating the right foods and replacing the nutrients lost with each swallow of an alcoholic beverage. In fact, they'll learn how to enjoy the high that comes from drinking without the sickly aftermath. *1999, 5½ x 8½, 213 pp, charts, indexed, soft cover.* $14.95.

☐ **85272 THE BIRTH OF HEROIN AND THE DEMONIZATION OF THE DOPE FIEND,** *by Th. Metzger.* In the collective American psyche, fearsomely addictive heroin and the deranged dope fiends who inject it have come to be associated with defilement, skin, disease, and a plethora of moral and physical transgressions. But this was not always the case, and this fascinating book traces heroin's history, from its discovery, through its worldwide usage and acceptance and to its eventual demonization. Today, heroin and its devotees have become synonymous with devolution and degeneracy. How this came to be is an engrossing tale, and this book provides a unique societal insight unlike anything you've ever read before. *1998, 5½ x 8½, 240 pp, soft cover.* $15.00.

❑ 88888 **Loompanics Unlimited 2001 Main Catalog, THE BEST BOOK CATALOG IN THE WORLD.** Over 800 titles listed. See our catalog ad at the end of this book. **$5.00.**

Please send me the books I have marked below.

❑ **85186, Opium for The Masses, $14.95**

❑ **40083, You Are Going to Prison, $14.95**

❑ **85203, Stoned Free, $14.95**

❑ **85212, The Politics of Consciousness, $18.95**

❑ **85346, Herbs of The Northern Shaman, $14.95**

❑ **94317, Sex, Drugs, & The Twinkie Murders, $19.95**

❑ **85293, Drink As Much As You Want And Live Longer, $14.95**

❑ **85272, The Birth of Heroin, $15.00**

❑ **88888, Loompanics Unlimited 2001 Main Catalog, $5.00, (*FREE* if you order any of the above titles.)**

Loompanics Unlimited
PO Box 1197
Port Townsend, WA 98368

HUH

I have enclosed $ _____ which includes $5.95 for shipping and handling of the first $25 ordered. I have added $1 for each additional $25 ordered. Washington residents include 8.2% sales tax.

Name _____

Address _____

City _____

State/Zip_____

We accept Visa, Discover, and MasterCard.
To place a credit card order call **toll-free 1-800-380-2230**,
24 hours a day, 7 days a week.
Check out our Web site: **www.loompanics.com**